PROSPERITY EDUCATION

IELTS Academic
Reading Practice

Sample Papers

Jane Turner

PROSPERITY EDUCATION
www.prosperityeducation.net

Registered offices: Sherlock Close, Cambridge
CB3 0HP, United Kingdom

© Prosperity Education Ltd. 2021

First published 2021

ISBN: 978-1-913825-50-8

This publication is in copyright. Subject to statutory exception and to the provisions of relevant collective licensing agreements, no reproduction of any part may take place without the written permission of Prosperity Education.

'IELTS' is a brand belonging to Cambridge Assessment English, the British Council and IDP: IELTS Australia, and is not associated with Prosperity Education or its products.

The moral rights of the author have been asserted.

Cover design and typesetting by ORP Cambridge

For further information and resources, visit:
www.prosperityeducation.net

To infinity and beyond.

Contents

Introduction			2
About the *IELTS Reading Practice: Academic Student Book*			3
Test 1	Passage 1	Matching headings; True/False/Not Given; Short answer questions	6
	Passage 2	Matching information; Choosing a title; Flowchart completion	9
	Passage 3	Sentence completion; Multiple choice	12
Test 2	Passage 1	Yes/No/Not Given; Summary completion; Multiple choice	18
	Passage 2	True/False/Not Given; Multiple choice; Table completion	21
	Passage 3	Matching information; Matching sentence endings; Short answer questions	24
Test 3	Passage 1	Yes/No/Not Given; Categorisation/classification; Table completion	28
	Passage 2	Matching headings; Summary completion; Multiple choice	31
	Passage 3	True/False/Not Given; Multiple choice; Categorisation/classification; Table completion	34
Test 4	Passage 1	True/False/Not Given; Multiple choice; Diagram completion	40
	Passage 2	Matching headings; Summary completion; Multiple choice	44
	Passage 3	Sentence completion; Choosing a title; Matching sentence endings; Short answer questions	49
Test 5	Passage 1	Matching headings; Yes/No/Not Given; Summary completion	54
	Passage 2	Multiple choice; Choosing a title; Flowchart completion; Short answer questions	57
	Passage 3	Sentence completion; Multiple choice; Categorisation/classification; Choosing a title	61
Test 6	Passage 1	Summary completion; Multiple choice; Matching sentence endings; Diagram completion	66
	Passage 2	Yes/No/Not Given; Matching information; Sentence completion; Multiple choice	70
	Passage 3	Matching headings; Multiple choice; Short answer questions	73
Test 7	Passage 1	Yes/No/Not Given; Choosing a title; Table completion; Short answer questions	78
	Passage 2	Matching headings; Sentence completion; Multiple choice	81
	Passage 3	Matching information; Summary completion; Multiple choice	85
Test 8	Passage 1	Yes/No/Not Given; Summary completion; Categorisation/classification	90
	Passage 2	Matching headings; Sentence completion; Multiple choice	93
	Passage 3	Yes/No/Not Given; Multiple choice; Short answer questions	96
Answer key			101

Introduction

There are two types of IELTS test – Academic and General Training. Some parts of each test (such as the speaking and listening sections) are the same. This resource provides exam-styled practice for the IELTS Academic Reading test.

Author **Jane Turner** is an associate lecturer in EAP/EFL at Anglia Ruskin University, Cambridge, and an EFL materials writer for international exam boards, universities and publishers. She previously worked as a Cambridge ESOL examiner for the British Council, and holds an MA in Education Management, and Cambridge CELTA and DELTA.

The tests in this book include the 15 different reading tasks that you may encounter during the IELTS Reading test:

1. Matching headings	6. Sentence completion	11. Matching sentence endings
2. True / False / Not Given	7. Multiple choice	12. Table completion
3. Yes / No / Not Given	8. Matching features	13. Flowchart completion
4. Matching information	9. Choosing a title	14. Diagram completion
5. Summary completion	10. Categorisation/classification	15. Short answer questions

The Academic Reading section tests a wide range of reading skills and strategies. Some tasks may involve **reading for gist** (i.e. general understanding, or overall meaning). Others may require you to **read for the main ideas** in a text. You might also need to **read for detail** or **specific information**. Or perhaps you will be required to read closely in order to **understand a logical argument** in a text.

In practice, many IELTS Academic Reading tasks test more than one of these skills at the same time. For example, you may need to understand the gist of a paragraph to establish whether it includes the information you are looking for. Then, you might need to look for specific information within that paragraph.

The Academic Reading test takes 60 minutes (including time to transfer answers to the answer paper), and includes three reading passages with a variety of questions and task types. There are 40 questions in total, and each answer is worth one mark. The reading passages are usually 700–800 words long, with 12–14 questions per text, and are taken from books, journals, magazines, websites and newspapers. They have been written for a non-specialist audience, and they may be presented in a variety of styles (e.g. discursive essays, descriptions, explanations, narratives, etc.). You should not worry about the subject of the text. Although you might prefer to read about familiar topics, you are being tested on your reading skills and not your subject knowledge. You do not lose marks for wrong answers, so you should always guess rather than leave blanks on the answer sheet. Spelling is very important.

The content of this resource has been written to closely replicate the IELTS exam experience, and has undergone comprehensive expert and peer review. We hope that you will find it to be a useful study aid, and we wish you all the best in preparing for the exam.

About the Student Book

IELTS Reading Practice: Academic is both a classroom and self-study resource written by expert IELTS teachers and authors. Each of the 14 units in this book introduces a different reading task that you may encounter during the IELTS Academic Reading test.

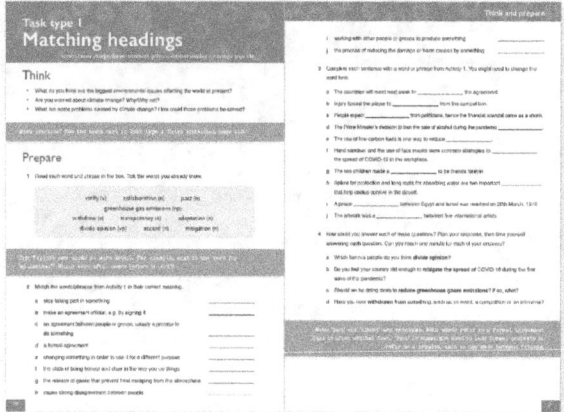

1. Think and prepare starts with some questions to get you thinking about the unit topic, and introduces some challenging words and phrases that will appear in the practice activities that follow.

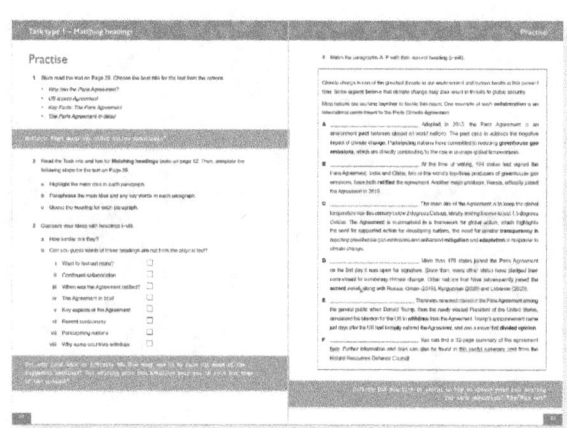

2. Practise introduces a new reading task for you to practise the task type using a text that is shorter than what will feature in the exam. It starts with some strategies and tips for how to approach each task, for you to try these strategies out during the activities then reflect on what went well, what you learned and what you will need to do to improve.

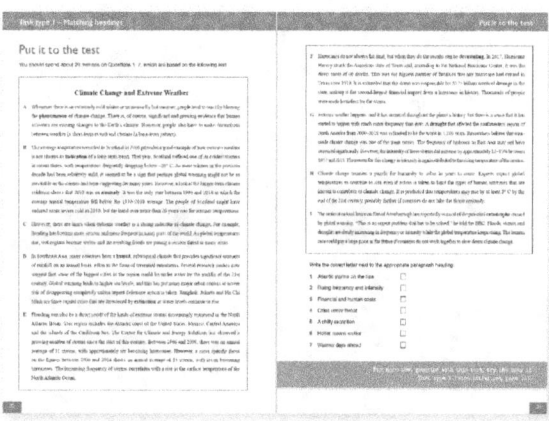

3. Put it to the test includes a text that is designed to replicate an IELTS Reading test task. There is no support here – it's just you, the text and the questions!

IELTS Reading Academic

Test 1

IELTS Academic Reading

READING PASSAGE 1

You should spend about 20 minutes on Questions 1–14, which are based on Reading Passage 1 on the next page.

Questions 1–5
Reading Passage 1 has 6 sections, A–F.
Choose the correct headings for Sections **A** and **C–F** from the list of headings below.
Write the correct number i–viii in answer boxes 1–5.

List of headings
i   Detecting lies and opportunities
ii The development of olfaction
iii Smelling for survival
iv Trends in perfume making
v   Smell and memory
vi The impact of smell in retail
vii The science behind creating popular scents
viii The complexity of smell

Example:

                Answer

1 Section B   *iii*

1 Section A

2 Section C

3 Section D

4 Section E

5 Section F

The Sense of Smell

Section A
Although we may take it for granted, our ability to smell, also called olfaction, has played a crucial role in human evolution. Olfaction enabled early humans to identify food sources, and differentiate between safe things to eat and those which were potentially harmful. Smell also helps reinforce vital blood bonds. Research has shown that humans develop an innate olfactory instinct within the womb. Unborn babies become familiar with the unique smell of their mother, meaning that when born, they can distinguish their caregiver from other adults. Likewise, mothers can instinctively recognise the so-called "odour cues" of their own baby. As a result, when faced with similar-looking infants, parents can identify their own offspring, thereby ensuring the safety of their baby. Would the human race have flourished as it has without olfaction?

Section B
In addition to detecting actual scents or odours, smell is the sense often associated with identifying hidden threats to our wellbeing. We don't literally use our nose to discover whether someone is being dishonest. Rather, we often refer to our feelings of suspicion or mistrust in smell-related terms, as the expression "to smell a rat" illustrates. Likewise, the idiom "smell blood" is used when we sense an opportunity to take advantage of someone we believe is in a weak position. Similar expressions exist in many other languages, suggesting that, compared to other senses, we may have a more emotional or even instinctive relationship with smell. This is just one aspect that arguably makes olfaction the most mysterious of the five senses.

Section C
Of course, humans now employ multiple senses when interacting with the world. In fact, much emphasis is now placed on sight and sound. Far more scientific research is conducted into these two senses, and, consequently, more is known about them. However, smell is far from being an inferior sense. For one thing, our sense of taste depends heavily on olfaction. What's more, although smell is one of the oldest of the five senses, it is far from the simplest. Our ancient sense of smell has always been remarkably sophisticated. For instance, while our eyes have just four light sensors to sense visual stimuli, the nose uses approximately four hundred different olfactory receptors. Such a large number of highly sensitive receptors enables the nose to identify an astonishing range of scents. In fact, researchers now believe that humans are capable of detecting at least a trillion different smells.

Section D
There are further differences between smell and other senses, especially in the way olfactory information is received and processed in the brain. Information about touch, sight or sound initially enters the brain through an area called the thalamus. However, smells are directly processed in a different area called the olfactory bulb, situated by the hippocampus. This area of the brain is involved in learning, long-term memory and emotion, and is necessary for remembering past events and experiences. The fact that only olfactory signals are processed near the hippocampus could indicate that smells are processed on a deeper, more emotional level compared to other types of sensory information. Some experts believe that recalling past experiences from sights or sounds leads to factual types of response. By contrast, odours can create intense emotional reactions, almost as if the smell transports us directly back to the past. This "smell nostalgia" can produce incredibly powerful feelings in us, especially if the memory is associated with someone we haven't seen for a long time.

Section E
The power of smell can even be exploited for commercial gain. One study found that shoppers may spend up to twenty minutes longer in a shop that smells nice, and that pleasant scents could increase the probability of a sale by up to eighty per cent on average. Similarly, the associations we have for certain scents can be used to make people feel certain emotions. That's why baking is a common tactic used when people are trying to sell their home. When potential buyers come to view the property, the smell of baking coming from the kitchen not only makes the home smell nice, but also conveys a sense of cosiness. Subconsciously, people entering the home will make the association with the pleasant scents and positive feelings about the property itself. This can make all the difference in property sales.

Section F
Then there is the perfume sector, which continues to see huge growth. One of the latest innovations has been the development of aromatherapy perfumes designed to enhance one's mood. What's more, luxury fashion houses can attract new customers by developing their own scents. Many consumers want to buy something associated with designer fashion without having to worry about the price. And just like clothing trends, specific perfume ingredients or perfume styles become fashionable at certain points in time. However, unlike clothing, perfume smells slightly different on every person. We all have our own unique skin chemistry, which means that the various ingredients in the perfume react in different ways on our skin. For this reason, no company has managed to create a scent with universal appeal. This again demonstrates our special relationship with smell.

Questions 6–11

Do the following statements agree with the claims of the writer in Reading Passage 1?

In boxes 6–11, write:

TRUE If the statement agrees with the information in the passage
FALSE If the statement contradicts the information in the passage
NOT GIVEN If there is no information on this in the passage

6 Humans' sense of smell starts to develop as soon as they are born.

7 Olfaction receives less academic attention than some other senses.

8 It is impossible to detect different smells without using taste receptors.

9 Sensory signals about smells and sounds are sent to different parts of the brain.

10 Visual memories produce stronger emotional responses than olfactory memories.

11 The use of smell can influence the average amount of money customers spend in shops.

Questions 12–14

Answer the questions below using **NO MORE THAN THREE WORDS** from the passage for each answer.

Write your answers in boxes 12–14.

12 Which phrase is mentioned as an idiom that is used to express a sense of doubt?

13 What is the minimum number of smells that experts believe the human nose can detect?

14 Which part of the brain is associated with remembering past events?

READING PASSAGE 2

You should spend about 20 minutes on **Questions 15–27**, which are based on Reading Passage 2 below.

Section A
Commercial farming has seen numerous changes over the years. For instance, agricultural innovations have made farming less labour-intensive, with tasks such as watering and planting crops becoming increasingly mechanised. Likewise, pest management has been transformed with the introduction of chemical pesticides and the development of genetically modified crops. While such developments have helped farms to increase crop yields, food security remains a key concern. Given the rising global population, farmers are struggling to meet the growing demand for affordable, safe produce. At the same time, the environmental impact of agriculture is under closer scrutiny than ever before.

Section B
Agriculture puts a strain on the environment in several ways. Farming requires a substantial amount of land, an issue of global importance as land becomes ever scarcer. Agriculture typically contributes to other important problems, too, such as soil erosion, loss of wildlife habitats and pollution. Environmentalists also point out that the carbon footprint of many forms of agriculture is considerable, as are the energy and water requirements of farming. For these reasons, scientists and growers strive to identify more ecologically sustainable ways to supply the world with fresh food.

Section C
In recent decades, the quest for environmentally friendly farming practices has largely centred on growing crops in town and cities. The development of vertical farming has played an important role in this. As the name suggests, this type of farming involves growing crops in vertical racks or shelves stacked on top of one another rather than planting them horizontally across wide open spaces. Vertical farms maximise urban space by making use of abandoned sites such as vacant apartment blocks, disused underground tunnels, abandoned mine shafts or old shipping containers. While vertical farming is still relatively new, its value has risen sharply. This market is forecast to be worth almost £10 billion within a decade.

Section D
Growing vertically is just one aspect that sets this form of farming apart from conventional agriculture. Another is that the crops are grown without soil. This can be done using a hydroponic growing method, where plants are grown in large trays or containers connected to a large water tank. Instead of taking nutrients from soil, the plants are fed a liquid solution. Using a water pump, the liquid is sent from the water tank into the containers at certain intervals, often regulated by an automatic timer. The liquid solution contains the essential nutrients needed for plant growth. Submerging only the roots of the plant in the solution prevents the plants from suffering damage from excess water. Once the container is full, the solution will overflow and drain back into the tank. The liquid remains there until the timer automatically activates the pump again. Thus, the mineral solution is circulated between the tank and the plant tray. The mineral composition of the solution can be adjusted to ensure plants receive the right amounts of nutrients.

Section E
Of course, plants also need light. In vertical farming, the crops are grown indoors and therefore have limited access to natural light. Therefore, artificial lighting must be used, and arranged in such a way that it can reach every layer of the plants. Placing a single powerful light source directly above the highest layer of plants could result in the top plants being overexposed to harsh light, while the trays of plants beneath them receive insufficient light. Fortunately, with advances in lighting technology, individual lighting units can be placed safely between each layer of plants. This ensures that all plants receive adequate light. In fact, modern LED lighting can be adjusted to generate lighting of different colours and intensity, meaning that it's possible to optimise the lighting specifically for each individual type of crop. Experts argue that this leads to greater control over when the plants flower and even how the crops will taste.

IELTS Academic Reading

Section F
Clearly, vertical farming makes use of ingenious techniques, and its growing number of supporters argue that it's vital for securing a sustainable food supply. Vertical farming is also relatively efficient in terms of its water requirements, meaning that far less water is used to grow plants. This is an important ecological advantage. In addition, since the crops are grown in areas where they don't have to travel so far to reach their end user, it's argued that this reduces the carbon footprint of agriculture. On top of this, the crop yields achieved by vertical farming methods are impressive, often beating those achieved by conventional farming. For example, one study found that twenty times more lettuce can be grown in vertical farms than in fields. Viewed from the perspective of the planet's diminishing land resources, this is an undeniable benefit, and one that is likely to become increasingly important.

Section G
Investment in vertical-farming technology is increasing. Nevertheless, claims that vertical farming is set to revolutionise agriculture may be a little premature. Unless the expense required to create vertical farms falls, it will remain too costly for most growers. This will prevent vertically farmed produce from being easily affordable. Moreover, many of the world's most popular crops cannot be grown easily using vertical farms. And while vertical farming does offer several ecological benefits, its green credentials can be disputed because of its extremely high energy consumption. Some of these obstacles may eventually be overcome, but it's unlikely that vertical farming will replace conventional farming entirely.

Questions 15–22
Reading Passage 2 has 7 paragraphs labelled A–G.
Which paragraph contains the following information?

*Write the correct letter **A–G** in answer boxes 15–22.*

NB: You may use any letter more than once.

15 evidence that vertical farms can produce high quantities of food

16 a financial prediction about the growth of the vertical-farming sector

17 an example of how a practical problem associated with vertical farming has been resolved

18 a description of how traditional farming can negatively impact nature.

19 an economic argument against vertical farming

20 a description of the locations used for vertical farming

21 an example of how scientific innovation has helped farmers protect their crops

22 a common method of feeding plants in vertical-farming systems

Questions 23–26
Complete the flow chart below.

Choose **NO MORE THAN TWO WORDS** from the text for each answer.
Write your answers in gaps 23–26.

Vertical farming: A hydroponic system

> In a hydroponic system, crops can be grown without using
> (23)_____.

↓

> Instead, plants are grown in containers that receive water from a
> (24)_____.

↓

> A liquid is regularly pumped into the containers. This solution contains
> (25)_____ that help plants grow well.

↓

> Since only the roots are in contact with the solution, the harmful effects
> of (26)_____ are avoided.

Question 27
Choose the correct letter, A, B, C, D, or E.
Which of the following is the most suitable title for Reading Passage 2?

Write the correct letter **A–E** in the answer box below.

A   How technology has helped make vertical farms more popular

B   Is vertical farming the key to sustainable food supplies?

C   Water and energy consumption in vertical farming

D   The practical limitations of vertical farming

E   How have vertical farms transformed urban environments?

IELTS Academic Reading

READING PASSAGE 3

You should spend about 20 minutes on Questions 28–40, which are based on Reading Passage 3 below.

New Directions: *Rita Lewis on the marvels of maps*

I've always been fascinated with maps. As a child, I spent hours exploring world atlases memorising the exotic names of all the faraway places that caught my imagination. I was intrigued by the tiny dots of remote islands, and imagined how long it would take to sail to such places, and what I might find there. As an adult, my interest in maps has become more practical. I use them as tools for planning holidays or days out. Maps showing the elevations of hills help me to identify suitable walking routes, while city maps highlight places of local interest. While I've always been curious about maps, only recently has my attention turned towards cartography.

The fact that early humans depicted their surroundings in cave paintings proves we've always sought to understand the physical world. In this sense, maps have existed for millennia. Some ancient maps showed the night sky rather than land features, presumably for navigational purposes. The first published world map is thought to have been the work of the ancient Greek philosopher Anaximander. While he is regarded as the "father of cartography", ancient Chinese cartographers were just as influential. They developed maps with gridlines and scales, which remains an important aspect of modern mapmaking. Jewish cartographers also played an important role by developing charts for navigation at sea. Cartography also owes much to individuals including Piri Reis, Al Idrisi and Fra Mauro. They mapped much of the world and set the foundations of the modern discipline.

It's incredible to think that much of our knowledge about the Earth was discovered using only simple instruments and handmade maps. For centuries, distances were calculated using ropes or chains of specific lengths. Over time, the development of basic instruments and tools helped cartographers and explorers to make their calculations with greater ease. For instance, compasses allowed cartographers to plot angles. Later, the introduction of small telescopes or magnifying glasses attached to these compasses made it easier to see two points that were far apart. Of course, compared with modern maps, many old maps were less detailed. However, given the fact that they were made without the aid of sophisticated digital tools, some of the most ancient maps in existence are remarkably accurate.

We shouldn't assume that inaccuracies on historical maps are the result of miscalculations. Sometimes cartographers intentionally misrepresented geographical features for valid scientific purposes. For instance, in the sixteenth century, the cartographer Gerardus Mercator produced a map which became known as the Mercator projection. As the map was designed to serve as a navigational tool for sailors, Mercator altered the shape and scale of the continents. He did this to make it easier to represent the curved shape of the world on a flat map. This enabled sailors to plot sea routes more easily. The Mercator projection has been extremely influential for centuries and while it isn't perfectly precise, it's still widely used.

Maps from the past also provide us with fascinating insights into the development of our world. Rather than showing physical geographical features like mountains or rivers, political maps focus on features of human geography, such as official boundaries or road systems. Such details can quickly become outdated through no fault of the cartographer. Therefore, such maps shouldn't be viewed as fixed representations of reality, but as records of how the world has been organised at certain points in history. Maps can reveal how the world was once perceived. For instance, ancient European maps often featured artistic elements and symbolic imagery. These illustrations were visual commentaries conveying positive or negative viewpoints about various places. This form of "cartographic propaganda" demonstrates that there is more to maps than geographic fact.

The role of maps extends far beyond presenting technical information in a systematic way. Anyone who has ever seen a beautiful, hand-drawn ancient map would surely accept that cartography's position on the art–science spectrum is open to debate. Cartographers have to keep in mind their intended audience, and the purpose of the product. Much like a cookbook, maps may be used to entertain and inspire as well as inform. Therefore, cartographers should consider not only geographical information, but also ease of use and attractive presentation. Thus, cartography incorporates both scientific and aesthetic elements.

Mapmaking continues to be a highly specialist field, combining technical skill, subject knowledge and an eye for detail. Of course, the mapmaking process has inevitably moved with the times. Modern cartographers have cutting-edge technology at their disposal, helping them to create maps which are as precise as possible. Thanks to digital mapping tools, maps now cover even greater detail than ever. For this reason, the days of struggling with a paper map in the wind and rain may soon be over, as we can consult maps directly on our phones. As this technology becomes widespread, people now entering the mapmaking profession are expected to be familiar with programming languages. Scientific innovations are also used to identify physical changes on the planet. For instance, as the consequences of climate change start to affect the Earth, satellite imaging is playing a key role in helping cartographers to identify areas where maps need to be altered. Unquestionably, mapmaking remains vital.

Questions 28–34
Choose the correct letter, A, B, C or D.

Write the correct letter **A–D** in answer boxes 28–34.

28 What does the writer say about her experience of maps?

    A Looking at maps has inspired her to visit unusual places.

    B She prefers studying cartography to looking at maps.

    C Over time, her main reason to look at maps has changed.

    D Her knowledge of the world is mainly due to looking at maps.

29 What contribution did early Chinese cartographers make to mapmaking?

    A They created a mathematical system of organising places on maps.

    B They produced the first complete maps of the entire world.

    C They produced the earliest examples of navigational maps.

    D They invented new instruments to produce maps.

30 In the past, cartographers used to measure the distance between points using a

    A telescope.

    B chain.

    C compass.

    D magnifying glass.

31 What point does the writer make about Mercator's maps?

    A Mercator's maps led sailors to make more mistakes.

    B Mercator knew there was inaccurate information in his maps.

    C Mercator made errors when calculating how big continents were.

    D Mercator's maps have become less popular nowadays.

IELTS Academic Reading

32 Political maps are an example of maps which

    A can be interpreted in different ways.

    B are designed to change people's attitudes about a place.

    C combine geographic and artistic features.

    D may go out of date over time.

33 The writer refers to the example of cookbooks to show that

    A the purpose of a publication may affect how it is presented.

    B there is little difference between art and science.

    C it is important to present technical information clearly.

    D artistic elements can improve the quality of a factual publication.

34 According to the text, satellite technology is particularly useful for

    A discovering new areas that need to be mapped.

    B making the mapmaking process more efficient.

    C correcting mathematical errors on earlier maps.

    D updating maps due to environmental changes.

Questions 35–40

Complete the sentences below with words taken from Reading Passage 3.

*Use **NO MORE THAN TWO WORDS** for each answer.*

Write your answers in boxes 35–40.

35 Early navigational maps depicted the …

36 Some charts that helped sailors navigate were originally created by …

37 A design that made it easier to represent the Earth's round shape on flat maps was the …

38 Using map design to influence people's opinions is a type of …

39 There are different opinions about whether cartography should be categorised as science or …

40 Working as a cartographer now requires knowledge of …

IELTS Reading Academic

Test 2

READING PASSAGE 1

You should spend about 20 minutes on **Questions 1–13**, which are based on Reading Passage 1 below.

Nudge Theory

We might assume that people make sensible, carefully considered choices at all times, but the truth is that humans don't always act in their own self-interest, or behave in perfectly rational ways. People make countless "snap decisions" or "impulse buys" on a daily basis, many of which may not be particularly smart choices. But what drives us to do this when just a few minutes' thought could prevent us from making unwise decisions?

Two different modes of information processing can drive people's behaviour. Humans certainly possess the ability to consider various options and draw conclusions. This involves consciously evaluating data and considering how the information fits in with their needs and desires. This type of cognitive reasoning should help us to avoid making poor judgements. To illustrate, making a supermarket shopping list means we are less likely to be tempted into wasting money on unnecessary items. However, there are situations in which this type of information processing has less influence on our actions.

Evidence suggests that our capacity for rational information processing is limited. Once the information required to make judgements becomes too complex or involves too much time to process, we are less likely to apply cognitive reasoning. This may result in no action being taken at all. For instance, making important financial decisions such as saving for retirement can seem incredibly complicated, which is why many people put it off. This is not because we lack the necessary information to make a choice. It is due to the fact that the decision requires the analysis of so many variables, and, consequently, we feel overwhelmed. And if we do make a decision, it may well be driven by a different type of information processing.

When people make choices while feeling under pressure or overwhelmed, their decisions are more likely to be made instantly at the subconscious level. In these circumstances, research has shown that we are heavily influenced by our external environment. If we're hungry, we're more likely to accept an offer of a biscuit even when we're trying to cut down on sugary snacks. Our impulsive desire for instant gratification takes priority over our rational understanding of healthy eating. Of course, reaching for the occasional biscuit isn't the end of the world, but it illustrates the fact that impulsive behaviour can hinder our ability to make the best decisions for our wellbeing.

But can our decision-making patterns be improved? Supporters of nudge theory certainly believe so. Proponents of this theory seek to harness the power of instant, subconscious processing in positive ways. Subconscious processing involves making quick decisions without cognitive reasoning, meaning we select the option requiring the least effort. According to nudge theory, in the right circumstances, external cues can actually help people automatically adopt the best course of action. By making the sensible option the easiest to select, people will hopefully choose it without even thinking.

Governments are making increasing use of nudge theory to influence citizens' behaviour in areas including energy consumption, healthy eating and financial planning. The key principle is that, by controlling the way various options are presented, people can be guided towards certain desirable actions.

One common way for governments to influence people's behaviour is by setting the target behaviour as the default option. As picking an alternative requires effort, most people naturally stick to the default option unless they feel strongly opposed to it. For instance, in many countries citizens are required to enrol if they wish to participate in organ donation programmes. In such countries, organ donation rates are low since people rarely make the effort to sign up. Several countries have addressed this by changing the default option to automatic registration on organ-donation programmes. Citizens are of course free to opt out, but they must make the effort to do so. Studies have shown that few people decide to leave the programme. This suggests that low registration rates in "opt in" countries are largely due to people not making the effort to sign up, rather than because of any objections to organ donation.

Behavioural nudges can also be applied by altering external cues. Research has shown that highlighting a particular option in comparison to others increases the likelihood that it will be selected. Thus, displaying healthier food items in prominent and easily accessible places in shops will make it more likely that customers will buy them. Similarly, people are thought to be influenced by other people's behaviour. If they see other people donating money to a charity collection, they will usually follow this example and do the same.

It is hard to argue against any measures designed with society's best interests in mind. Nevertheless, concerns have been expressed about nudge theory's manipulative nature. Critics argue that it potentially interferes with people's civil liberties, especially if alternatives to the intended behaviour are made virtually impossible to access. Ethical concerns aside, some people have questioned whether nudges lead to long-lasting changes. While there is compelling evidence that people can be tempted into making certain choices in an instant, studies have yet to prove that they will continue to adopt that behaviour permanently.

Questions 1–8
Do the following statements agree with the claims of the writer in Reading Passage 1?
In boxes 1–8, write:

> **YES**   If the statement agrees with the claims of the writer
> **NO**   If the statement contradicts the claims of the writer
> **NOT GIVEN** If it is impossible to say what the writer thinks about this

1 People often overestimate how much time is needed to make sensible decisions.

2 Cognitive information processing is associated with careful deliberation.

3 Insufficient information is the main reason why people postpone decision making.

4 Subconscious information processing results in quick responses.

5 Nudge theory encourages people to adopt cognitive reasoning.

6 Low organ-donation rates are mainly due to ethical concerns.

7 Defaults have been found to be more influential on people's decisions than external cues.

8 Evidence supporting nudge theory mainly focuses on its short-term effects.

Questions 9–12
Complete the summary using the list of words or phrases, A–I, below.
Write the correct word, **A–I**, in gaps 9–12.

Understanding Nudge Theory

We are less likely to make **(9)**_____ when we feel stressed or confused. When our decisions are made using **(10)**_____, we generally prioritise immediate rewards over ultimate aims. However, altering the way "nudges" are presented to people can change this. For instance, there has been a clear **(11)**_____ in organ-donor registrations in countries where citizens have to take action to opt out of the programme. Even so, there is doubt concerning the **(12)**_____ of nudge theory.

A	long-term impact	B	logical decisions	C	behavioural nudges
D	statistical evidence	E	increase	F	subconscious processing
G	fall	H	cognitive reasoning	I	defaults

Question 13
What is the writer's purpose in Reading Passage 1?
Choose the correct letter, A, B, C or D.

Write the correct letter **A–D** in the answer box below.

A   To argue that people often overestimate how much time is needed to make sensible decisions

B   To show that cognitive information processing is associated with careful deliberation

C   To analyse whether insufficient information is the main reason why people postpone decision making

D   To defend the idea that subconscious information processing results in quick responses

READING PASSAGE 2

You should spend about 20 minutes on Questions 14–27, which are based on Reading Passage 2 below.

Motoring Trends

The 1950s saw significant economic expansion in many developed countries. Several governments launched ambitious infrastructure programmes, including substantial investment in road networks intended to serve the needs of the growing urban and suburban communities. At the same time, manufacturing innovations enabled companies to produce large quantities of goods at more affordable prices. This meant that more households could buy products that had previously been beyond their means. In particular, car ownership became something that more people could finally achieve, and it became both attainable and desirable. Cars became a practical necessity, enabling more people to reach the growing employment opportunities in cities. They also opened up new leisure possibilities, leading to growth in the tourism sector. Thus, cars have played a key role in economic development in the second half of the twentieth century.

Motoring trends attract considerable research interest. Academics in various fields analyse car sales to forecast potential changes in car-ownership rates. Much like housing trends, vehicle-usage patterns can reveal valuable insights into how lifestyles are changing. Likewise, car-ownership trends may reflect people's attitudes to consumption and social status. They can also be a useful indicator of a country's economic conditions, demographics and population distributions. In a wider sense, policy makers have to understand the implications of changing transportation trends. This helps governments to decide whether to invest more in roads, public transport or cycling routes, and helps climate scientists to make vital forecasts about air-pollution levels.

Studies on motoring trends in developed countries indicate that car ownership is currently in decline. Car sales are falling, and analysts have also found evidence that car usage is decreasing. Compared to previous decades, fewer people are applying for driving licences or taking driving tests. Motorists are also driving shorter distances, and cars are seemingly becoming less popular in many developed nations including Germany, the UK and the USA. Is this the death of the motor car?

Different models have been used to examine motoring trends. One approach focuses on the impact of economic conditions. When there are significant changes in a country's gross domestic product (GDP), fewer people may be able to afford major purchases such as a car. This GDP-based approach could explain why car ownership has risen in emerging economies such as India and Russia. Viewed from this perspective, the current falls in car usage in countries such as the UK or Germany should be regarded as temporary decreases rather than permanent downward trends. This "interrupted growth" will end once the economy improves. Provided this happens, car usage and car sales will rise.

However, many analysts doubt that the motor industry is destined for further growth as the car market may have become saturated. In economics, market saturation occurs when demand for a product has stopped increasing: anyone who has the ability and intention to buy the product has already done so, therefore the market can no longer attract new customers. To illustrate, a recent study investigated car-ownership patterns in American households, and found that, on average, there were more cars per household than drivers. This means that many households already have more cars than they actually need. Therefore, it is probable that car usage will remain constant in the coming years, but new consumers are unlikely to enter the market.

Some experts have gone further and support the "peak car" hypothesis. This hypothesis states that vehicle usage has already reached its maximum, and will therefore gradually and permanently decline. "Peak car" isn't linked to an ability to supply the needs of the motor industry. Rather, it is concerned with a perceived decline in demand for cars as societies cease to be organised around motor travel. According to this theory, there has been, or will soon be, a fundamental shift in the role of cars in society.

Supporters of the peak car theory argue that, as nations develop, people will rely less on car travel. Consequently, the distance travelled in private cars will decrease, as will car-ownership rates. Research suggests that most people are unwilling to travel more than an hour on a single journey per day. This is known as people's "travel budget". Recent studies have found no noticeable change in the amount of time people are prepared to spend travelling to complete their daily tasks. However, improvements in technology, public transport and local amenities mean that it's becoming increasingly possible to meet one's needs without

IELTS Academic Reading

spending an hour in a car. Furthermore, the growth in car-sharing smartphone apps means that people no longer view cars as desirable objects to own, but as something to be hired instantly when needed for short journeys.

Personal convenience is not the only factor influencing people's attitudes to cars. Environmental concerns are undoubtedly affecting the automotive sector. Growing awareness of the need to reduce carbon emissions has influenced legislation in many countries, which has led to greater commitment to public transport. Motorists are also opting for car models which are thought to be more environmentally friendly, as demonstrated by the growth of electric- and hybrid-car sales in recent years.

While the world may not be ready to give up cars entirely, our love affair with them is fading.

Questions 14 and 15
Chose **TWO** letters, A–E. Write the correct letter A–E in answer boxes 14–15.

*The list below gives some reasons why the middle of the twentieth century was an important time for economic growth in many countries. Which **TWO** of these reasons are mentioned by the writer of the text?*

A   Rural areas received financial support from governments. — 14

B   The price of consumer goods fell significantly. — 15

C   The number of people entering the job market increased.

D   The travel and tourism industry developed.

E   The quality of consumer goods improved.

Questions 16–18
Chose **TWO** letters, A–F. Write the correct letter A–F in answer boxes 16–18.

*The list below gives some reasons why experts analyse motoring trends. Which **THREE** of these reasons are mentioned by the writer of the text?*

A   Motoring trends can potentially affect environmental issues such as pollution. — 16

B   It helps the motor industry forecast which models are likely to be popular. — 17

C   Rising car sales can significantly improve national economies. — 18

D   It can help governments decide which transport policies to prioritise.

E   Motoring trends are closely linked to people's housing choices.

F   It provides evidence of how society is evolving.

Questions 19–23
Complete the table below.
Choose **NO MORE THAN TWO WORDS** from Reading Passage 2 for each answer.
Write your answers in gaps 19–23.

Explanation	Examples / evidence	Predicted car usage trends
GDP-based approach	Rising car sales in emerging markets such as Russia and India	Car usage will grow if the (19)_____
Saturation point	Multiple cars in (20)_____	There is unlikely to be further growth in demand for new vehicles Car usage is likely to (21)_____ in the coming years
(22)_____ theory	Growth of car ride apps	Both car ownership and (23)_____ in cars are likely to decline

Questions 24–27
Do the following statements agree with the claims of the writer in Reading Passage 2?
In boxes 24–27, write:

    TRUE   If the statement agrees with the information in the passage
    FALSE   If the statement contradicts the information in the passage
    NOT GIVEN If there is no information on this in the passage

24   The number of driving licence applications has fallen in some countries.

25   Private vehicle usage rates are similar in Germany and the USA.

26   The length of time people are willing to spend on daily journeys has decreased.

27   Environmental concerns are influencing the types of cars consumers are purchasing.

READING PASSAGE 3

You should spend about 20 minutes on **Questions 28–40**, which are based on Reading Passage 3 below.

Stage Arrangements in Theatre

Section A
Whether planning a musical comedy or serious drama, theatre producers must consider many creative elements to achieve their dramatic objectives. For instance, visual elements can enhance the performance space. This area of theatre production, known as stage design, is mainly concerned with how lighting, props and costumes support the performance.

However, before these additional elements can be planned, producers must consider the physical arrangement of the performance space itself. Wise use of stage layout can have a surprisingly powerful effect on the overall impact of a performance. Conversely, failing to take it into consideration can ruin the efforts of performers and stage designers. In the most extreme cases, issues with stage layout may make the action onstage difficult to see or feel very artificial, leaving audiences underwhelmed.

Section B
The position of the stage and performers in relation to the audience can be arranged in various ways, each with pros and cons. Different arrangements may be selected to create a particular atmosphere, or to influence how audiences and actors interact during a performance. For this reason, certain types of staging are often associated with different types of show or dramatic genre.

Of course, practical constraints can determine the stage layout just as much as artistic preference. Producers may be forced to use a certain type of arrangement because no other option is available. For instance, in old theatres with fixed seating, it's virtually impossible to change the layout of the performance space. Therefore, understanding the individual strengths and weaknesses of a particular stage layout helps producers to identify the creative elements which are most likely to work.

Section C
When most people picture a live theatre performance, they usually imagine actors performing on a raised rectangular stage facing rows of seated audience members. This classic style, the proscenium stage, became popular during the Italian Renaissance, although its origins can be traced back to ancient Rome. This layout places performers directly in front of the audience. Actors enter and exit from several different directions, including the side wings or from the back of the stage.

The key feature of this arrangement is the proscenium, or proscenium arch. This physical structure serves as a kind of picture frame or window through which the performance is viewed. It focuses the audience's attention towards only what is meant to be seen onstage. In this sense, the proscenium provides both a literal and figurative separation between the performance area and audience.

Section D
For centuries, theatres were designed around the principles of proscenium staging, and this has become a standard theatrical layout. Many renowned theatres make impressive use of this design. When accompanied by beautiful background scenery, dramatic lighting and a live orchestra, the overall effect can be extremely powerful. On a practical level, since the entire audience is seated facing in one direction, everyone usually has a clear view of the action, with nothing blocking lines of sight. A further benefit is that lighting can be stored in an area above the stage called the flyspace, away from the audience's view.

However, depending on the size of the theatre itself, audiences may feel quite far from the stage. This, combined with the fact that there is relatively little scope for the performers to move around, can make the action feel artificial. Therefore, alternative types of staging may be preferred to achieve an intimate, natural connection between audience and performers.

Section E
If the aim is to make the audience feel more directly involved in the action, a theatre-in-the-round format can be extremely effective. In this layout, also known as arena staging, the performance area is in the centre, with the audience seating arranged around it. Actors enter using walkways placed between audience seating. This builds up the excitement as the actors move through the audience towards the stage. Arena staging brings the audience closer to the action, which can be particularly useful for productions which require participation from the spectators.

However, it's important to ensure that the performers move around the stage frequently so that they address different sides of the audience throughout the show. Otherwise, some audience members will only see the performers' backs during the performance. Similarly, the placement of lighting and scenery must be planned so that it doesn't interfere with actors' sight lines when they change directions.

Section F
An even more dynamic type of staging is promenade theatre, where it's the audience that moves rather than the performers. The action takes place across multiple sites, or "stations". Actors remain in their individual stations and, when the audience arrives, they perform their scene, after which the audience travels to the next one. This format can certainly create an immersive experience. It's often a highly engaging way of bringing factual information to life, which is why the format is commonly used in interactive museum and city tours.

However, more than any other type of staging, this format has many uncontrollable variables, since the performance only begins once the audience reaches the site. If the distance between sites is too great, the rhythm of the show will be affected, and the audience may even forget what has already happened. From a safety perspective, the route between stations must be carefully planned. Planning any live performance involves consideration of safety matters, but with promenade staging, the risks are greater since it involves the movement of so many people.

Section G
Ultimately, logistic, artistic and budgetary factors influence how theatre companies present their work. No staging format is without challenges or limitations. Nevertheless, selecting the right format does more than support the performance. In the best cases, it can actually add an extra dimension which enhances the dramatic impact of the story.

Questions 28–33
Complete each sentence with the correct ending A–J from the box below.
Write the correct letter **A–J** in answer boxes 28–33.
N.B. You may use any letter more than once.

28 Stage design in theatre production

29 Choice of stage layout

30 The proscenium stage arrangement

31 A lack of connection between audience and performers

32 During in-the-round productions, some of the audience

33 Consideration of safety matters

A	is considered to be a traditional type of stage layout.	F	is one potential drawback of proscenium staging.
B	is mainly determined by the number of actors on the stage.	G	is likely to be distracted by lighting.
C	has particular importance when organising promenade productions.	H	has restricted views of the performers unless the action onstage is carefully planned.
D	focuses on incorporating visual elements to enhance live performance.	I	involves a greater range of practical difficulties than other theatre formats.
E	is the main advantage of promenade staging compared to proscenium staging.	J	affects the type of interaction actors and spectators have during a show.

IELTS Academic Reading

Questions 34–37
Answer the questions below using **NO MORE THAN THREE WORDS** from the passage for each answer.

Write your answers in boxes 34–37.

34 During which historical period did proscenium staging gain widespread attention?

35 What can be kept in the flyspace?

36 What do actors use to get to the stage in arena layouts?

37 Which type of staging involves the audience moving from place to place?

Questions 38–40
Reading Passage 2 has 7 sections labelled A–G.
Which paragraph contains the following information?

Write the correct letter **A–G** in answer boxes 38–40.

NB: You may use any letter more than once.

38 a popular belief about how theatre shows look

39 an example of an educational application of theatre staging

40 an explanation of what stage designers do

IELTS Reading Academic

Test 3

READING PASSAGE 1

You should spend about 20 minutes on Questions 1–14, which are based on Reading Passage 1 below.

The Charity Sector

The serious business of good intentions

A sense of purpose isn't the only requirement when it comes to working in the charity sector. While charities undoubtedly aim to help society, they make strategic decisions just like any other business. Therefore, charities cannot rely on the support of enthusiastic volunteers alone. In fact, that's a very small part of the sector. Charities employ professionals in areas including IT, marketing, and finance. And recent graduates no longer view working for a charity as a temporary option before starting a private-sector career. As recruitment expert Tim Callahan explains, "Charities are becoming more market-driven. They realise they have to compete with the corporate world to attract the best individuals. Salaries are rising to reflect this."

An essential activity for all charities is fundraising. While some charities generate revenue by selling their own products, they still depend mainly on donations. Without this financial support, charitable organisations simply wouldn't be able to operate. But, of course, charities have to stand out from other organisations doing similar activities. Like selling any other product or service, charity fundraising is about finding the right strategies to persuade people to part with their money. From friendly volunteers collecting donations on the street on behalf of a good cause to professional fundraisers pitching their organisation's work to potential corporate sponsors, knowledge of marketing techniques can make all the difference.

Effective communication is the key to selling anything. With charity fundraising, there are several messages that organisations have to convey. First, they have to demonstrate the need for their work, which means raising awareness of a particular problem in society. Then they need to demonstrate how the charity's work has a positive impact in this area. This "problem–solution" model is used to sell products in numerous sectors including health and beauty, household cleaning or kitchen appliances. However, because of the highly sensitive nature of the information that charities need to convey, these organisations have to communicate their message extremely carefully.

The concept of "emotional contagion" is a fundamental principle of charity advertising. Essentially, when people are presented with happy images, they feel positive, whereas sad images create negative emotions. Therefore, showing sad images such as sick children or mistreated animals can be a powerful way to raise awareness of a problem. According to psychology lecturer Dr Laura Highmore, such images can encourage people to donate to a charity: "When charities use images that focus on suffering, it communicates that the situation is urgent or very serious. It's natural for people to experience feelings of guilt or sadness when they see these images. Consequently, they're more likely to donate immediately because they want to stop these uncomfortable emotions. That's why the 'sad face' strategy often appears in charity advertising."

However, several studies have shown the limitations of the "sad face" strategy. While it can attract donations from people who don't usually give to charities, it can actually have the opposite effect on frequent donors. Miriam Freeman, a researcher of charitable giving, suggests that seeing such images makes people feel their donations are having little impact. Therefore, they may feel there's no point in continuing to support charities. For such audiences, charities need to communicate their "emotional contagion" message in a different way. Research has shown that when charities focus on the positive impacts of their work using happy images, the satisfaction levels of their donors increase. As a result, they feel even more engaged with the organisation. As Richard Banks, marketing coordinating at a healthcare foundation explains, "It's about reassuring our donors that their contributions directly support the essential work we do."

A recent survey in the UK revealed that, while retail accounted for almost 40% of all charitable donations amongst adults over 30, younger people preferred to donate via events such as concerts. Although these only accounted for 10% of total contributions, charities aiming to attract younger donors should bear this in mind.

Overall, cash was the most popular payment method, accounting for just over half of all payments. This suggests that people make spontaneous donation decisions. By contrast, only 2% of all contributions are deducted directly from staff salaries. Charity analyst Joseph Butler predicts that this will grow in popularity because charities are focusing increasingly on this in their marketing. Similarly, direct debits which come out of a person's bank account on a regular basis are extremely valuable to charities as they guarantee a stable source of income. At present, these payments make up a quarter of all charity contributions, but this is another trend which is likely to become more important to charities.

Inevitably, some charitable causes will always be more popular than others. While this is entirely natural, it means that some charities struggle to gain attention or funding. Some people argue that, just like any other market, only the strongest charities should survive. Others claim that governments should use charitable donations as a way of determining which causes are most important to the public, and plan their policies accordingly. However, both of these viewpoints ignore the fact that all charities make positive contributions to society. Governments should support any organisation that strives to make the world better.

Questions 1–8
Do the following statements agree with the claims of the writer in Reading Passage 1?
In boxes 1–8, write:

YES   If the statement agrees with the claims of the writer
NO   If the statement contradicts the claims of the writer
NOT GIVEN   If it is impossible to say what the writer thinks about this

1 Charities rely mainly on volunteers to make up their workforce.

2 People working for the private companies earn more than those working in the charity sector.

3 Charities make more money from donations than from their own commercial activities.

4 Charity advertising is different from advertising in retail.

5 The "sad face" strategy is the tactic most frequently used in charity advertising.

6 How often a person usually donates affects how they respond to emotional fundraising campaigns.

7 Charity concerts are most popular with young people.

8 Governments should prioritise helping smaller charities.

IELTS Academic Reading

Questions 9–12
Look at the following statements (Questions 9–12) and the list of people in the box below. Match each statement with the correct person A–D.

Write the correct letter **A–D** in answer boxes 9–12.

NB: You may use any letter more than once.

9 People who donate to charity on a regular basis may be discouraged by negative images.

10 Positive images reinforce the value of donating to charity.

11 Perceptions of work in the charity sector have changed.

12 The way people donate to charity is likely to change.

| **A** Tim Callahan | **B** Miriam Freeman | **C** Richard Banks | **D** Joseph Butler |

Questions 13 and 14
Complete the chart below.

Choose **NO MORE THAN TWO WORDS** from Reading Passage 1 for each answer.

Write your answers in gaps 13–14.

UK DONATIONS BY TYPE

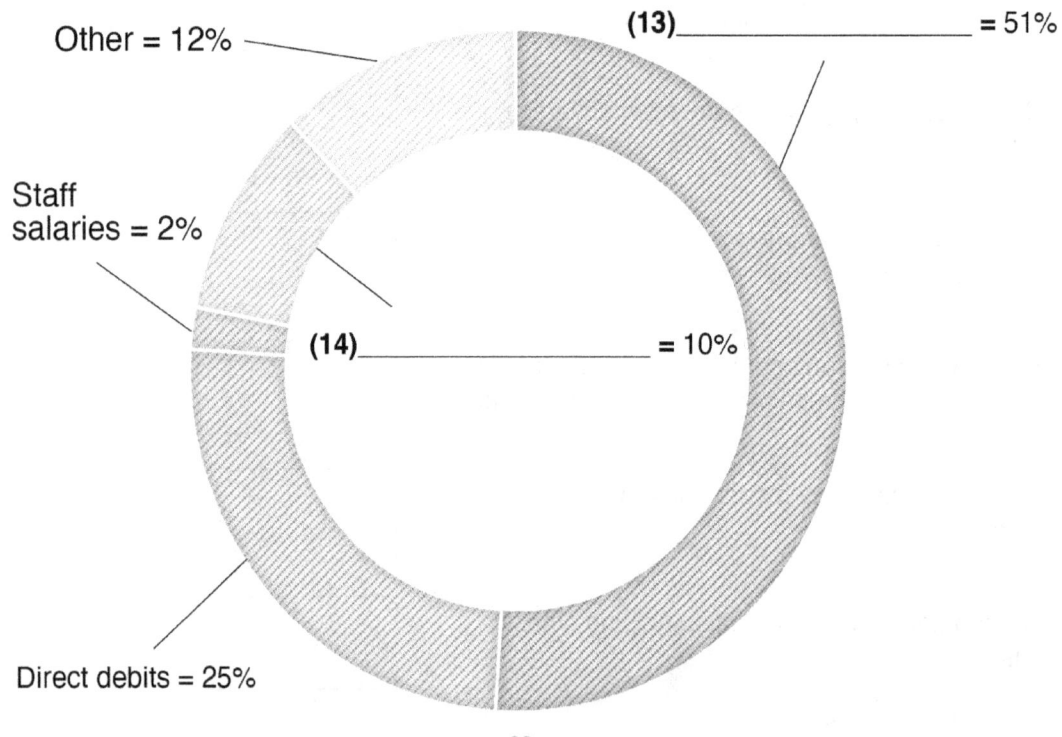

Other = 12%
(13) _____ = 51%
Staff salaries = 2%
(14) _____ = 10%
Direct debits = 25%

READING PASSAGE 2

You should spend about 20 minutes on Questions 15–27, which are based on Reading Passage 2 on the next page.

Questions 15–19
Reading Passage 1 has 6 sections, A–F.
Choose the correct headings for Sections **A** and **C–F** from the list of headings below.
Write the correct number i–viii in answer boxes 15–19.

List of headings

i   A world of choice
ii Appointment TV
iii Targeting mainstream audiences
iv The focus on interactive TV
v   Instant gratification
vi Too much of a good thing?
vii Meeting viewers' needs

Example:

                Answer

Section **B**   *ii*

15 Section A

16 Section C

17 Section D

18 Section E

19 Section F

IELTS Academic Reading

Screen Time

This week, it's the turn of writer Paul Meyers to share his views about TV

Section A

My friends and I are poles apart when it comes to our TV-viewing preferences. Not so much in terms of the programmes we enjoy, more in the way we watch them. Typically, my friends stream shows using on-demand services on their devices so that they can watch whatever they want whenever they like. Nothing wrong with that of course, but they insist on "binge-watching" episode after episode so that they finish an entire series in one afternoon! Personally, I can't see the appeal of viewing shows in this way. Why is there such a drive to get everything immediately nowadays? Why can't people wait? After all, who wants to eat a whole box of chocolates all at once?

Section B

My friends tease me for what they regard as my old-fashioned attitude to TV. For me, nothing beats watching shows as they're actually broadcasted on TV, especially when it's a drama with an intriguing plot. Making the effort to tune in each week for the latest instalment is part of the fun. Waiting to discover how the story will unfold builds the anticipation. Best of all, it also gives viewers the chance to swap theories about what might happen next. I like the idea of the entire audience following along at the same time, with all the viewers experiencing the plot twists at the same moment. Just like watching a match at the stadium, it's a shared experience for people to discuss afterwards. I miss the days when conversations would begin with: "What did you think about last night's episode?" You don't get that when all the episodes are available at the click of a button!

Section C

Even so, I understand that TV needs to move with the times. In fact, I welcome the way broadcasters have evolved to respond to viewers' desire for flexibility. Channels realise there are many different forms of entertainment at our disposal, all competing for our attention. And it's not just teenagers that feel this way. With all this choice, people are less likely to commit to watching something at a fixed time each week. For this reason, the idea of "must-see" TV that everyone tunes in to watch at the same time is fast becoming a thing of the past. Instead, many channels now offer online "catch-up" services so that viewers can log in and watch their favourite shows on any device at a time that's more convenient. This is invaluable given how busy most people are nowadays.

Section D

And of course, TV channels now face increasing competition from commercial subscription services, such as those my friends use for their TV-viewing marathons. For a monthly fee, customers gain access to a wide variety of programmes of every genre to suit all tastes. With these services, subscribers can watch programmes from all around the world, rather than just those shown in their home country. From Japanese anime to Brazilian soap operas, commercial streaming platforms enable people to watch programmes that they wouldn't have been able to access previously. This is obviously an attractive proposition for programme makers as it opens up new markets for their output. As these streaming platforms grow in popularity, it'd be nice to think that audiences will become more open-minded and adventurous in their viewing habits. I'd certainly applaud anything that encourages people to explore different cultures.

Section E

But are viewers actually getting as much choice as they assume? In theory, these on-demand services offer almost unlimited opportunities for audiences to broaden their viewing horizons. In reality, whenever a viewer finishes watching something, the platform subtly directs them toward watching more of the same by recommending a similar show. From a commercial perspective, this makes sense. After all, these sites have a business model which is all about retaining customers. They're more likely to do this by constantly updating their range of popular shows that appeal to the broadest range of viewers rather than by trying to meet everyone's individual specialist tastes. For this reason, these services offer a wide rather than deep selection of programmes. As far as I can tell, while it's possible to find shows of every genre, the variety within each category is limited unless the genre has mass appeal.

Section F

Still, these subscription services do enough to keep viewers generally entertained even if they can't offer an extensive library of niche or unusual programmes. What concerns me is the general move towards viewer participation in TV shows. People no longer passively watch a programme. Instead, they're encouraged to get involved in some way. For instance, there are far too many TV competitions or reality shows where viewers vote to eliminate a contestant each week. These shows are relatively cheap to produce. I suspect that's far more of a consideration than TV companies' claims that interactive programming makes the audience more emotionally invested. Surely, true audience engagement comes from making high-quality shows with interesting characters and unpredictable plots? If that's no longer the focus, maybe it's time I switched off altogether!

Questions 20–23
Choose the correct letter, A, B, C or D.

*Write the correct letter **A–D** in answer boxes 20–23.*

20 What does the writer suggest about his friends?

   A They have poor taste in TV shows.

   B They are difficult to please.

   C They lack self-control.

   D They dislike new trends.

21 According to the second paragraph, the writer most enjoys

   A predicting the plot of TV dramas.

   B watching TV when he's with other people.

   C live sport broadcasts.

   D TV shows that require little effort.

22 What point does the writer make about TV channels?

   A They are focusing too much on young audiences.

   B They are adapting to suit modern lifestyles.

   C They are becoming less popular.

   D They are improving their range of programmes.

23 What is the writer's attitude towards commercial TV subscription services?

   A Impressed with the convenience they offer

   B Hopeful that they will improve the quality of TV programmes

   C Concerned that they encourage people to watch too much TV

   D Doubtful that they offer as much variety as people believe

Questions 24–27

Complete the summary using the list of words or phrases, A–I, below.

Write the correct word, **A–I**, in gaps 24–27.

TV Trends

It is clear that the way people want to **(24)**_____ TV programmes is changing, with viewers expecting to have instant access to programmes on a range of devices. And while traditional TV stations have started to offer **(25)**_____ options, they face competition from newer services which customers pay to access. In theory, the main selling point of these newer commercial platforms is the **(26)**_____ of their programming. For instance, they are exposing audiences to **(27)**_____ content they might not have been able to watch before.

A	subscription	B	consume	C	cheapness
D	variety	E	series	F	broadcast
G	catch-up	H	traditional	I	international

READING PASSAGE 3

You should spend about 20 minutes on Questions 28–40, which are based on Reading Passage 3 below.

Introduction

The link between technology and learning has been the focus of considerable academic study in recent decades. For instance, there has been a wealth of research comparing the impact of traditional face-to-face education with that of online learning. Similarly, as laptop computers become increasingly widespread, there have been numerous studies analysing their impact on learning. While computers certainly bring students a range of benefits, research has revealed certain limitations of these devices. For example, some researchers have found evidence suggesting that the use of laptops can negatively affect students' ability to concentrate. Students are more likely to be distracted when using these devices to complete tasks in class.

Electronic notetaking

While the pros and cons of using laptops in school classrooms continue to be debated, electronic notetaking has become standard practice in many higher-education contexts. University students are often required to take comprehensive notes during lectures, and there is a common perception that typing information on a keyboard is simply more convenient than writing by hand. Typing takes less time and mistakes can be instantly corrected on the screen. Most documents can be automatically checked for spelling or grammatical errors, which is undoubtedly another positive when it comes to editing one's work. Paragraphs can be re-ordered with just a click or swipe, without having to re-write anything. In addition, electronic information can easily be stored and transferred to other devices.

It is clear then that electronic notetaking offers several practical advantages over writing by hand. However, previous research has cast doubt on whether this type of notetaking can actually support learning. For instance, one notable study at an American university found that students who took notes by hand could remember more about what they had learned compared to students who had taken notes on their laptops. The researchers also reported higher test scores amongst students who used handwritten notes to prepare for their assessment compared to students who had prepared for the test using electronic notes.

Another finding from the American study concerned the different notetaking strategies employed by students when writing or typing information. Based on their analysis of students' notes, the researchers concluded that, when taking notes on a laptop, students tend to type down far more of the lecture word by word. By contrast, taking notes by hand encourages students to be more selective about what they write, and summarise the key points in their own words. This appears to suggest that, while electronic notetaking is an effective way of recording information accurately, it may impair learners' ability to focus on the meaning of the information.

The study
Our study replicated the aims of the American research, but this time focused on the context of an undergraduate literature class. Literature undergraduates are expected to move beyond pure memorisation. The content of lectures is typically less fact-based, focusing instead on the discussion of broad themes and concepts. As such, we wanted to see whether electronic notetaking may have an impact on the types of notes students take in a degree subject which requires considerable analytical and critical thinking.

In our study, eighty participants took notes during a series of literature lectures. The lecture content was designed to ensure that it was unfamiliar to all the students. This was so that no participant would have an advantage due to previous exposure to the topic. Students were randomly assigned to either Group A or Group B. Students in Group A made and stored all their lecture notes using laptops, while students in Group B took their notes by hand.

After the lectures, the students' notes were analysed. The aim was to ascertain whether the two groups differed in their notetaking strategies. The notes were examined in terms of how much of the lecture the students had noted down, how closely their notes resembled what was said during the lecture, and whether the students had added their own comments or analysis of the lecture content.

Findings
Analysis of the students' notes confirmed the findings of the American study. Participants using laptops noted down far more of the lecture compared to the Group B students. The electronic notes included even minor details, often reproducing the exact words used by the speaker. By contrast, students taking notes by hand focused on the key themes of the lecture. Their notes included more paraphrases, and contained more of the students' own comments. This suggests that the Group B students were analysing the content while they were writing.

Discussion
Based on this and earlier studies, it would appear that students adopt different strategies depending on whether they are taking notes electronically or by hand. Taking notes by hand seems to encourage students to focus more on understanding the ideas rather than recording every detail. Further research is needed to determine the extent to which this may impact upon students' academic success, although it seems likely that handwritten notes may be more useful when studying conceptual information rather than facts. It is also worth investigating whether students are aware of how to take effective notes.

IELTS Academic Reading

Questions 28–31
Choose **FOUR** letters A–G. Write the correct letter A–G in answer boxes 28–31.

The list below gives some advantages of using electronic devices in educational contexts. Which **FOUR** of these advantages are mentioned in the passage?

A   It helps students to stay focused.

B   It enables students to correct their mistakes easily.

C   It makes education more interesting for students.

D   It means students can organise their writing easily. ☐ 28

E   It is a convenient way for information to be stored. ☐ 29

F   It teaches students valuable online research skills. ☐ 30

G   It helps students to note down information easily. ☐ 31

Questions 32–36
Complete the table below.
Choose **NO MORE THAN TWO WORDS** from Reading Passage 3 for each answer.

Write your answers in gaps 32–36.

Previous research	Present study
Focus on the impact on learning	Based on a previous study conducted at an (32)_____
Previous studies have compared traditional classroom-based lessons and (33)_____	Investigated notetaking strategies of students studying (34)_____
Studies suggest that computers may make students more (35)_____ in class	The researchers made sure that the topics of the lectures were (36)_____ to all the participants

Questions 37–39
Do the following statements agree with the claims of the writer in Reading Passage 3?

In boxes 37–39, write:

TRUE If the statement agrees with the information in the passage
FALSE If the statement contradicts the information in the passage
NOT GIVEN If there is no information on this in the passage

37 The American study showed that electronic notetaking improved students' ability to recall information from lectures.

38 Group A students performed better in their university exams than Group B students.

39 Notes taken by hand have been found to contain more examples of students' own reflections.

Question 40
Choose the correct letter, A, B, C, D, or E.
Which of the following is the most suitable title for Reading Passage 3?
Write the correct letter **A–E** in the answer box below.

A A study comparing electronic and handwritten notetaking amongst university students

B A review of the different uses of laptop computers in university education

C The importance of teaching university students different notetaking strategies

D A case study of the academic impacts of electronic notetaking

E Comparing different types of electronic devices for notetaking in university lectures

IELTS Reading Academic

Test 4

IELTS Academic Reading

READING PASSAGE 1

You should spend about 20 minutes on Questions 1–14, which are based on Reading Passage 1 below.

Sounds Good!

Rory Mitchell explains how to turn our digital music files into superior sounds

Digital music

The vast majority of audio recordings we listen to nowadays are in digital formats, such as MP3 files. These compressed files are extremely convenient to use. Their small size means MP3 files can be downloaded easily and quickly, and thousands of them can be stored on computers.

The MP3 format also enables us to create a portable collection of our entire music collection. While many of us save our MP3 files directly onto our computers, it's always a good idea to back up files onto a portable memory stick, or USB drive. This means that we have access to our music collection should the worst happen and our computer develops a fault. This makes MP3 far more practical than older formats such as CDs.

However, like most things in life, there is a compromise to be made for all this convenience. The trade-off is the poor sound quality of digital audio files. To appreciate why this is, it's important to understand how sound works. The sound coming from a musical instrument or a person singing is nothing more than vibrating air. Microphones convert this movement of air into a variable electrical signal, otherwise known as an analogue signal. During the recording process, the analogue signal is converted into digital information. In order for us to be able to listen to that recorded music, we need equipment to convert it back to analogue. Our phones and laptops contain Digital to Analogue Converters (DACs) that do this but they tend to be poor quality. This negatively affects the quality of what we hear. Of course, this isn't an issue if you simply want to listen to music on your phone while sitting on the bus, but you can certainly hear the limitations of digital audio files when you play them through high-quality hi-fi equipment.

Although it's possible to play MP3 files on hi-fi equipment by plugging in your phone or laptop, the result will be nowhere near as good as it could be due to the limitations of your device's DAC. This means that, no matter how expensive your hi-fi system, you won't be able to enjoy the full range of the music as the artist intended. It's like filling a sports car with low-quality fuel – it'll still work but you won't be able to appreciate the potential of the car.

Fortunately, help is at hand, as it's relatively easy to convert digital MP3 files into high-quality analogue output which can be enjoyed on your hi-fi stereo system.

Can I use my laptop?

It's certainly possible to use your laptop computer to convert digital files into analogue signals, but the end result will still be disappointing when it's attached to your sound system. Most laptops have only a very basic internal DAC which is not powerful enough to function effectively with a hi-fi sound system. A good-quality DAC makes it easier to pick out all the individual sounds and tones of the music, resulting in a richer listening experience. This is the key to achieving the excellent sound quality that you seek from your stereo equipment. One option might be to buy a separate external DAC that can be attached to your laptop. However, external laptop DACs can be extremely expensive. In any case, if your computer is running other programmes or is updating while it's attached to your hi-fi system, the music playback is likely to be disturbed.

Instead, it's well worth investing in a single board computer (SBC) onto which you can instal a high-quality DAC. Both SBCs and their DACs are extremely cheap so for little extra expense, you can have a dedicated machine for audio purposes. Whatever you decide, the process of converting digital MP3 files into analogue sound to be played on your stereo is straightforward.

Data processing

First, insert your USB of MP3 files into the computer. All MP3 files consist of two types of data, processed by the computer in different ways. Data tags, containing information such as the song name, are sent to and displayed on the screen. For instance, when you attach a SBC to your TV, you will be able to see which song you are listening to. The audio data, which is the music recording itself, is sent to the DAC. The DAC accurately converts the digital audio into an analogue signal.

Amplification and output

Once the audio data has been converted, it is sent from the DAC to the hi-fi system, where it is amplified. Amplification involves taking a small analogue signal and making it much larger. This makes the signal more powerful. Finally, the amplified analogue signal is fed to the hi-fi speakers. This signal travels through a coil in the speaker which converts the electrical energy into a mechanical motion, which is why speakers vibrate.

With these steps in place, you can sit back and enjoy the way music is supposed to sound on a hi-fi system. I guarantee that, once you've heard the sound quality that can be achieved, you'll fall in love with your music collection all over again!

Questions 1–4

Answer the questions below using **NO MORE THAN THREE WORDS** from the passage for each answer.

Write your answers in boxes 1–4.

1. How is sound defined in the passage?

2. What type of device does the writer recommend instead of a laptop?

3. During which process is the analogue signal increased?

4. Which part of a hi-fi speaker creates vibrations?

Questions 5–8

Do the following statements agree with the claims of the writer in Reading Passage 1?

In boxes 5–8, write:

YES	If the statement agrees with the claims of the writer
NO	If the statement contradicts the claims of the writer
NOT GIVEN	If it is impossible to say what the writer thinks about this

5 Microphones transform sound into analogue signals.

6 Expensive computers have better DACs.

7 Sound quality can be improved with a more powerful DAC.

8 There are three types of data found in MP3 files.

Questions 9–11

Choose **THREE** letters A–F. Write the correct letter A–F in answer boxes 9–11.

The list below gives some reasons why MP3 digital files are popular. Which **THREE** of these reasons are mentioned by the writer of the text?

A MP3 files are simple to download.

B MP3 recordings are cheap to purchase.

C MP3 files are less likely to be damaged than CDs.

D MP3 files are extremely portable.

E MP3 files take up little storage space on computers.

F MP3 files are easy to record using basic equipment.

Questions 12–14
Complete the diagram below.

Choose **NO MORE THAN TWO WORDS** from the passage for each answer. Do not write articles (a, an, the).

Write your answers in gaps 12–14.

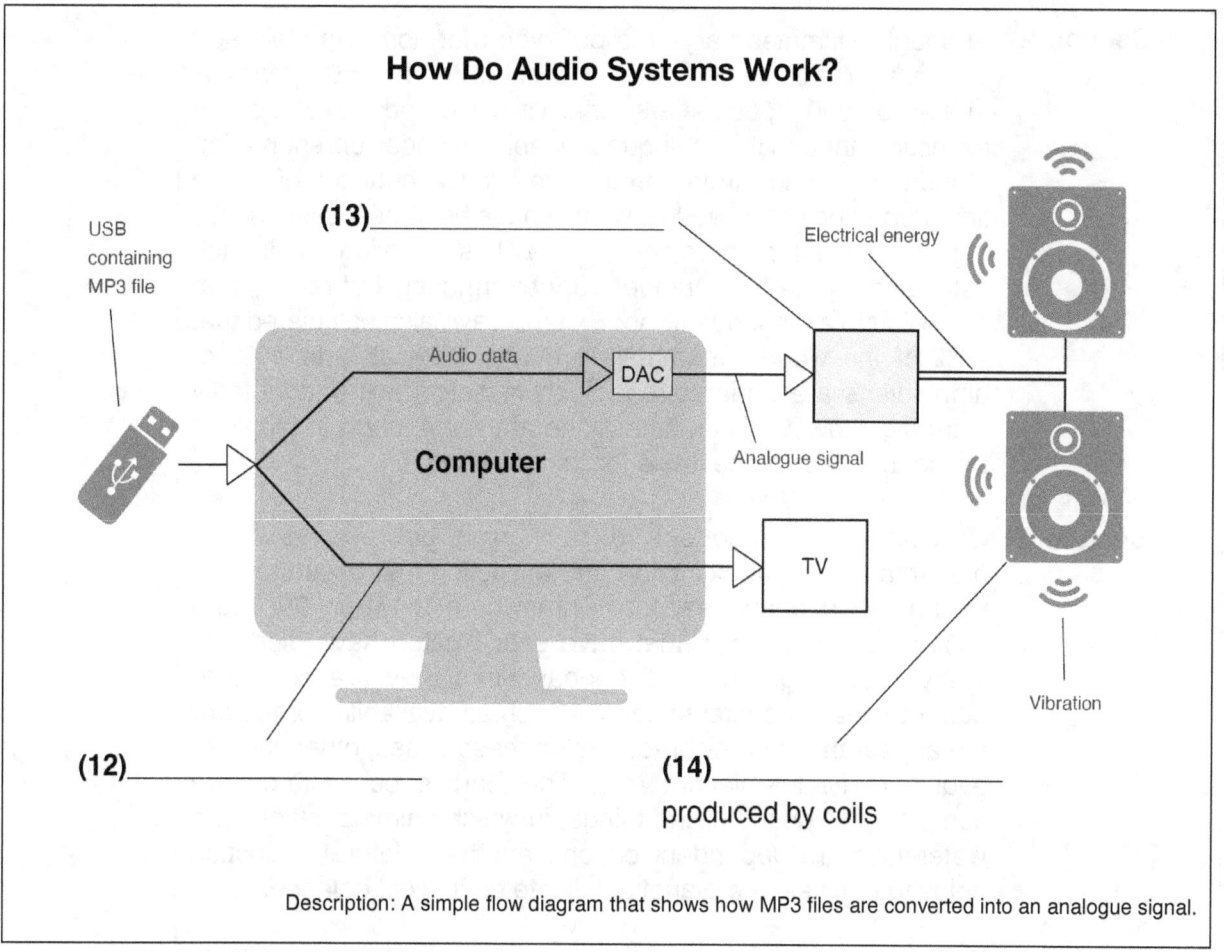

Description: A simple flow diagram that shows how MP3 files are converted into an analogue signal.

READING PASSAGE 2

You should spend about 20 minutes on Questions 15–27, which are based on Reading Passage 2 below.

Conservation Strategy

Section A Although estimates vary, it is believed that approximately 900 different animal species have died out in the last 500 years. A further 35,000 species are officially recorded as at risk of extinction, though this is unquestionably an underrepresentation of the true number under threat. The survival chances of only a tiny proportion of the world's wildlife have been assessed, so it's highly likely that far more species are at risk of dying out. In fact, estimates on the true number vary enormously but range from 10 million to almost 50 million. Experts have also calculated that 25% of the world's mammals are under threat, and 40% of amphibians are endangered. Such statistics are undoubtedly alarming. However, numbers alone are not enough to highlight the seriousness of the issue, or the solutions.

Section B Of course, it's important to distinguish between cases of preventable animal extinction and extinction that occurs due to natural evolutionary reasons. Somewhere between 90% and 99% of all the species that have ever existed have died out. Many species gradually disappear when they are unable to adapt to changing circumstances such as availability of food or the appearance of new predators. In these cases, other species evolve to fill the vacant role. The Earth's ecosystems are complex networks of living things, in which animals, plants and waterways are dependent on one another. Natural extinction helps to maintain the planet's delicate ecological balance.

Section C When left undisturbed, nature finds a way to restore itself. However, the natural balance of the world's ecosystems is changing, leading to significant biodiversity loss. Construction, tourism, mining, manufacturing and other aspects of human life are responsible for much of the environmental destruction we see in the world nowadays. Such activities directly lead to the loss of natural habitats, increase pollution and soil erosion, and also play a major role in climate change. All of this is having a disastrous impact on the planet's wildlife. Species are disappearing at rates estimated to be between 1,000 and 10,000 higher than rates of natural extinction. There's no doubt that humans have a disproportionately negative impact on the world. What's less clear is how best to resolve this.

Section D Wildlife management is far from straightforward, especially given the fact that it requires vast financial resources. To put this in context, it has been estimated that it costs over a million dollars a year to save just one single species of condor bird native to one particular area of North America. Since there are currently fewer than four hundred of these endangered condors in existence, saving each one comes at a cost of over $2,500 a year. With this in mind, wildlife management often involves weighing up competing environmental needs, and making painful strategic decisions to prioritise some species over others. The factors influencing such decisions are extremely complex, and often controversial.

Section E In recent years, the concept of "conservation triage" has gained increasing attention. This involves leaving some species to face extinction in order to allocate more resources to species with a greater chance of survival, or which are perceived to be more important in some way. Conservation triage recognises that it makes sense to invest our limited resources in species that will have the best environmental outcomes. However, there is no accepted formula to evaluate the relative merits of saving one species over another. The lack of consensus regarding which species should be prioritised means that wildlife agencies often adopt differing approaches when it comes to conservation efforts.

Section F Some conservation strategies focus entirely on "flagship" species. These are animals promoted as icons to raise public awareness of environmental issues. They are selected on the basis that they are commonly regarded as attractive or charismatic, and therefore valued in society. For instance, the possibility that the beloved giant panda may become extinct has highlighted the importance of protecting natural habitats and having tighter controls against deforestation. However, while cute animals may generate public sympathy, there is little evidence that this leads to significant environmental gains. In fact, if images of flagship species appear too often in marketing, the public may even assume they are no longer endangered.

Section G Although flagship species may be "cute", the arguments for alternative approaches are more compelling. It surely makes more sense to prioritise species which make the greatest overall contribution to nature, regardless of whether they are perceived to be attractive. Keystone species perform essential functions in ecosystems. For instance, elephants in the wild clear pathways for small animals. Insects and bees are essential for the pollination and dispersal of tree and plant seeds. Should keystone species disappear, the survival of all the forms of life in that environment would be at risk. Likewise, indicator species are vital as they provide valuable information about the condition of natural habitats. Some types of crayfish are used as indicator species. By monitoring crayfish populations, ecologists can understand more about the overall condition of our waterways. This clearly highlights the need for a pragmatic rather than a sentimental approach to conservation.

IELTS Academic Reading

Questions 15–20
Reading Passage 2 has 7 sections, A–G.
Choose the correct headings for Sections **A–C** and **E–G** from the list of headings below.
Write the correct number i–viii in answer boxes 15–20.

List of headings
i   Helpful species
ii   Humanity's ecological footprint
iii The complexity of conservation
iv   The extent of the problem
v   Ranking species
vi   Species as symbols
vii The failure of wildlife conservation
viii A natural phenomenon

Example:

                Answer

Section D   *iii*

15   Section **A**

16   Section **B**

17   Section **C**

18   Section **E**

19   Section **F**

20   Section **G**

Questions 21–23

Choose the correct letter, A, B, C or D.

Write the correct letter **A–D** in answer boxes 21–23.

21 The purpose of the second paragraph is to

   A highlight how species extinction could be prevented.

   B argue that species extinction is a growing issue.

   C compare the rates of preventable and natural forms of extinction.

   D explain how it is natural for many species to become extinct.

22 The passage mentions the condor bird as an example of a creature that

   A has been successfully saved from extinction.

   B is relatively expensive to protect.

   C has been prioritised over other species.

   D is a threat to North American native species.

23 What aspect of conservation does the writer support?

   A Focusing on protecting species that serve important purposes.

   B Encouraging the public to get involved in environmental programmes.

   C Using public opinion to determine how to allocate conservation resources.

   D Focusing on emotional arguments in conservation marketing campaigns.

IELTS Academic Reading

Questions 24–27
Complete the summary below. Chose **NO MORE THAN TWO WORDS** from the passage for each answer.

Write your answers in gaps 24–27.

Conservation Strategies

When the financial resources required to protect species from extinction are **(24)**_____, difficult decisions have to be made about how best to use these funds. There is now growing acceptance that such choices should be made based on the best long-term environmental prospects of the planet, an approach known as **(25)**_____.

One way to determine which species should be prioritised for conservation is by considering their overall impact on ecosystems. For instance, **(26)**_____ species directly help maintain ecosystems in numerous ways, such as by distributing seeds which ensures that plants continue to grow.

However, it's impossible to deny that we often hold more affection for some species compared to others, simply because they are more attractive. This can be used as a way of bringing attention to the need for conservation. A case in point is the fact that the **(27)**_____ has been used to raise awareness of environmental issues.

READING PASSAGE 3

You should spend about 20 minutes on **Questions 28–40**, which are based on Reading Passage 3 below.

About us: For over two hundred years, Havermore Academy has been at the forefront of linguistic research and language instruction. We are renowned not only for the quality of our teaching, but also our world-class facilities and innovative programmes.

The Havermore approach: At Havermore, flexibility is the key. With the exception of our full-time Language Teaching programme, which is delivered entirely at our beautiful campus, Havermore students have the option to combine campus learning with remote study, or take their courses completely online.

Havermore Academy offers undergraduate and postgraduate courses which are unparalleled in the scope and depth of their content. As well as our full degree programmes, we provide online foundation courses and access to one hundred supplementary language modules covering thirty different languages. All Havermore students are entitled to take one supplementary language module per semester at no extra cost. These supplementary language modules add further value to the Havermore experience, granting students the opportunity to learn an additional language from scratch.

Many of our programmes also offer participants an option to obtain official accreditation from professional bodies. These are additional qualifications that can be taken alongside the Havermore programme. Please refer to the Academic Office for more information about fees for professional accreditation.

Flagship postgraduate programmes: Havermore is particularly well regarded for its postgraduate degrees. Our three main masters' programmes are in Forensic Linguistics, Translation and Interpreting. Graduates from these programmes go on to highly successful careers in a diverse range of fields including criminal justice, international relations, publishing and international business. Although these three programmes are distinct in content and focus, they all include the compulsory module "Sociocultural Frameworks of Linguistic Analysis", in which participants explore the various factors shaping written and spoken communication.

Forensic Linguistics

Forensic linguistics is a relatively new branch of applied linguistics, and concerns the application of linguistic knowledge and methods to contexts such as criminal investigation and legal process. Forensic linguists analyse spoken and written discourse to identify patterns and characteristic traits to build a stylistic profile or "fingerprint" that can be used for investigative purposes. Our masters' course trains participants in the analytical skills required to examine spoken and written language in a range of specialist contexts. A unique feature of the course is the compulsory work placement that students take in their final semester. This enables students to gain valuable, real-life professional insights. Although the course is primarily intended to develop participants' practical skills, it also provides a solid theoretical foundation should students wish to pursue an academic-research career rather than field-based work.

Translation and Interpreting

Havermore Academy has been running its Translation and Interpreting postgraduate programmes for decades, and in this time we have trained interpreters and translators specialising in fifty different foreign languages. Our graduates use their foreign-language expertise to embark on rewarding careers working with leading international organisations, corporations and policy makers. Applicants wishing to enrol onto either of these programmes will be expected to have native or near-native proficiency in at least one foreign language. The level of expertise and skill required from these professions means that translating and interpreting are rarely undertaken by the same individuals. Understanding the key differences between the two fields will help you to identify the right programme for your needs and interests.

Translators work solely with written texts and documents. They typically convert written materials from a foreign language (the source language) into their native language (the target language). This requires extremely high attention to detail since translators must be able to convey the precise meaning and stylistic tone of the original source text. Many translators specialise in particular fields such as medical, technical, literary or legal translation. Harvermore Academy offers specialist optional modules in these fields as part of the masters' course. Prospective students intending to specialise in one of these areas will be required to demonstrate prior subject knowledge of their chosen field, typically through their undergraduate degree or evidence of prior relevant work experience. Students wishing to specialise in a particular area will be required to indicate this before commencing their programme.

Interpreters work with spoken language, often in two directions: translating from the source language into the target language and vice versa. As well as fluent speaking skills, interpreting involves a high level of listening comprehension, notetaking skills and the ability to make instant linguistic decisions. Although accuracy is important, interpreting does not require the same level of precision as translation, since the focus is on summarising and explaining the main message of what is being said. The fast-paced, dynamic aspects of interpreting make it a stimulating career for people who are confident working in high-pressure situations. As with the Translation course, applicants may choose to specialise in a particular area of subject knowledge. Unique to the Interpreting course is the opportunity to specialise in sports interpreting, a reflection of the increasingly global nature of professional sport.

Contact us: For in-depth syllabus information about our courses, please consult the relevant faculty pages on our website, or contact our Academic Office. We welcome applications from local and international students, and bursaries are available for applicants who can demonstrate outstanding academic credentials. These bursaries cover tuition fees.

Questions 28–34
Complete each sentence with the correct ending A–J from the box below.
*Write the correct letter **A–J** in answer boxes 28–34.*
N.B. You may use any letter more than once.

28 Translation applicants wishing to focus on a particular area of expertise

29 Students taking the Language Teaching programme

30 Obtaining an award from an official professional body

31 Studying sociolinguistics

32 Students studying for a Masters' in Interpreting

33 The Forensic Linguistics course

34 Proficiency in a foreign language

A	is primarily focused on research-based careers.
B	is a required aspect of the Translation course.
C	must be able to demonstrate prior knowledge of their intended subject.
D	develops students' ability to analyse and notice linguistic patterns.
E	may have the possibility to take a module concerning professional sport.
F	are not eligible to apply for financial bursaries.
G	do not have the possibility of studying their course online.
H	should expect to complete substantial amounts of coursework.
I	is one of the oldest courses offered by Havermore Academy.
J	is an optional aspect of some Havermore programmes.

Questions 35–39
Answer the questions below using **NO MORE THAN THREE WORDS** from the passage for each answer.

Write your answers in boxes 35–39.

35 How many different foreign languages are offered in the supplementary language programme?

36 What do all Forensic Linguistics students have to do in their final semester?

37 Which course trains students to work with written texts in a source language?

38 In addition to the website, where can students find information about Havermore courses?

39 What do students need to have in order to receive a bursary?

IELTS Academic Reading

Question 40
Choose the correct letter, A, B, C, D, or E.
Which of the following is the most suitable title for Reading Passage 3?

Write the correct letter **A–E** in the answer box below.

    A Invest in your future at Havermore Academy

    B Why study a foreign language?

    C Training to be a language teacher

    D Student life at Havermore Academy

    E Career opportunities for linguistics graduates

IELTS Reading Academic

Test 5

IELTS Academic Reading

READING PASSAGE 1

You should spend about 20 minutes on Questions 1–14, which are based on Reading Passage 1 on the next page.

Questions 1–6
Reading Passage 1 has 6 sections, A–G.
Choose the correct headings for Sections **A–C** and **E–G** from the list of headings below.

Write the correct number i–viii in answer boxes 1–6.

List of headings
i   The long-term impacts of horror
ii   Trends in horror
iii Widespread popularity
iv   Personal preference
v   Horror and identity
vi   Emotional highs and lows
vii A cultural icon
viii A genre like no other

Example:

                            Answer

1 Section D   *vi*

1 Section A

2 Section B

3 Section C

4 Section E

5 Section F

6 Section G

Scary Movies

Paula Johnson explores the horror genre

Section A
The horror genre is often derided by cinema critics as being artistically inferior to other types of film. They see little creative merit in films that are mainly intended to shock, repulse and terrify their audiences, a point reflected in the fact that horror films rarely win major industry awards. Yet, despite their lack of critical recognition, horror films have enjoyed significant commercial success for decades. And a strong case can be made that no other film genre attracts such loyal or dedicated audiences as horror does. There are cinema festivals, award ceremonies and fan conventions all devoted to the genre, and there's no sign that interest in horror is declining.

Section B
Although horror films may not be to everyone's taste, it's hard to ignore their impact on mainstream culture. The plot devices and cinematic techniques employed in horror films are instantly recognisable. Scenes and characters from classic horror films have become so iconic that they are widely known even amongst audiences with no interest in the genre, and they have been used as a source of inspiration in fashion design and music videos. In fact, the distinctive features of horror films are so familiar that they are often exploited for humour in comedy shows and even in advertising.

Section C
While devotees may defend the cinematic quality of horror films, there is substantial evidence that this is not the main reason why they appeal to so many people. Horror films evoke a range of different emotional responses in viewers, both positive and negative. Research indicates that these responses may be more powerful than the feelings viewers experience while watching other film genres. In other words, both the type and strength of emotions viewers experience while watching horror films simply cannot be replicated by other types of film. It is this unique feature of the horror genre that seems to be key to understanding its appeal.

Section D
But why exactly do people actively seek out the intense emotions associated with horror films? Several theories have been proposed, and many of these focus on the "tension resolution" aspect of most horror films. Horror films typically present situations designed to scare the audience or place them under great stress. Yet, at the end of the film, the plot is usually resolved with the hero somehow managing to escape from danger. Therefore, the audience's positive emotions at the end of the film are heightened because of the extreme stress and fear they had previously felt during the film. Much like a rollercoaster, we feel adrenaline and excitement because of the perceived danger. In addition, some psychoanalysts argue that watching horror films enables people to release their negative emotions, in much the same way that playing violent video games is thought to help people get rid of their aggression.

Section E
Many viewers derive pleasure from imagining themselves in the film and deciding what actions they would take. Viewers can challenge themselves mentally and emotionally without actually coming to any real harm. It is also worth noting that horror films tend to be rated more favourably by viewers when the hero is perceived as authentic. If the hero is someone with whom the viewers can identify, the audience will care more about the hero's struggles. Some studies even suggest that gender may play a role in people's perceptions of the characters in horror films. Although gender has not been conclusively found to influence whether someone enjoys horror films, it may play a role in determining how much empathy viewers have for the various characters in the films.

Section F
The horror genre includes various sub-categories, from extremely bloody, violent films to psychological thrillers and "cat-and-mouse" chases between good and evil. Some films cover classic supernatural themes such as haunted houses. In others, threats come from a human source. As with many other aspects of popular culture, the popularity of the genre has gone in cycles. For instance, zombie films were particularly fashionable in the 1960s and later in the early 2000s. In the 1980s, horror films focused more on the so-called "slasher" format, featuring a killer on the loose. The historian David Skal asserts that horror films are a reflection of society's main fears or concerns. Viewed from this perspective, contemporary zombie films could be interpreted as representing our concerns about widespread environmental destruction or fears concerning global threats.

Section G
When it comes to understanding audience's motivations for consuming horror films, I find sociological interpretations less persuasive than psychoanalytical perspectives. Ultimately, our decision to watch a horror film is a matter of personal taste, just as some people opt for romantic comedies or musicals. Whether our motives stem from the desire to be exposed to danger in a controlled way or a need to release negative emotions, horror films will continue to find enthusiastic audiences.

Questions 7–10

Do the following statements agree with the claims of the writer in Reading Passage 1?

In boxes 7–10, write:

YES If the statement agrees with the claims of the writer
NO If the statement contradicts the claims of the writer
NOT GIVEN If it is impossible to say what the writer thinks about this

7 Popular culture has been influenced by horror films.

8 Horror fans are mainly attracted to the superior quality of filmmaking in this genre.

9 Horror films which include sympathetic characters attract larger audiences.

10 The popularity of the horror genre is best understood by considering sociological factors.

Questions 11–14

Complete the summary using the list of words or phrases, A–I, below.

Write the correct word, **A–I**, in gaps 11–14.

Horror Films

Within the film industry, horror movies are rarely **(11)**_____ for their artistic quality. Instead, they are viewed as inferior to serious dramas or other cinematic genres. Yet this has not **(12)**_____ the high level of recognition the genre has achieved across society. The **(13)**_____ look and feel of horror films can often serve as a source of inspiration across various forms of mainstream culture.

Psychological and sociological theories offer competing explanations of what **(14)**_____ people to watch frightening content. However, like any other artform, an interest in horror is surely a matter of personal taste.

A	diminished	B	watched	C	familiar
D	influences	E	widespread	F	inspired
G	motivates	H	praised	I	enables

READING PASSAGE 2

You should spend about 20 minutes on Questions 15–27, which are based on Reading Passage 2 below.

Plastic has transformed the retail sector. The introduction of plastic containers and packaging has made the production and distribution of goods cheaper and more convenient, which has undoubtedly benefitted manufacturers, retailers and consumers. However, the widespread adoption of plastic has also been a major factor in the development of linear economic systems. A linear economy is a system based around a "take–make–discard" approach to resource management. In other words, raw materials are collected to produce objects which are only used once before being discarded. The vast majority of this waste cannot be recycled, and, in most cases, it is disposed of in ways which can harm the environment. And as societies have embraced single-use plastic, the resultant waste has become a serious problem which simply cannot be ignored.

It's clear that plastic waste endangers the lives of both land-based and marine wildlife. Toxic chemicals in plastic are extremely dangerous when ingested, which is something many creatures do by accident, as they often mistake small plastic items in their habitats for food. Discarded plastic packaging poses another threat to small animals since these creatures may get trapped inside plastic wrappers, and become unable to escape. Plastic waste also blocks drains and sewage systems, increasing the risk of flooding. These issues, along with the associated problems of secondary microplastic pollution, litter and carbon emissions, are driving many campaigners to demand a plastic-free future.

Many governments are attempting to address the issue by focusing on the thin, single-use plastic bags provided by shops and supermarkets. Approximately 130 countries have already restricted the use of these bags, presumably because it is one of the simplest ways to reduce the amount of plastic in the environment. Over 80 countries have implemented some form of plastic bag ban, while many others now impose a plastic bag tax, meaning that shops are required to sell the bags to customers rather than provide them free of charge. In many instances, governments use the revenue raised from the sale of plastic bags to fund environmental programmes such as cleaning up coastal areas.

As described in a report published by the United Nations, developing countries lead the way in terms of implementing complete plastic bag bans. Of course, it's worth noting that many of these countries are directly affected by plastic waste mismanagement. In fact, some of them are dealing not only with their own domestic plastic waste, but also the plastic waste coming from other parts of the world. As a result, these countries are already experiencing consequences such as serious flooding. By contrast, affluent countries, many of which export their plastic waste abroad, often impose less stringent measures. But regardless of why governments choose one particular measure over another, the question remains: are the policies working?

Many countries have reported substantial reductions in plastic bag usage after implementing restrictions. For instance, plastic bag bans in several municipalities in the Philippines have contributed to decreases in overall plastic waste collection. In addition, over 90% of citizens now use their own reusable grocery bags there. Likewise, after introducing charges for plastic bags, Portugal reported a 74% reduction in the consumption of plastic bags, along with a 61% increase in the usage of re-usable plastic bags. Such statistics are encouraging, but there are notable exceptions where measures have been less successful. Research has found that India did not enforce its ban effectively, which meant its impact on consumers' actions was minimal. In California, local regulations meant that retailers switched from providing plastic bags to offering paper bags. This actually encouraged people to use more bags to pack their groceries, leading to more waste overall.

Some environmentalists are unconvinced that targeting single-use bags is the right strategy to tackle global plastic waste. Although a paper published by Lund University states that a trillion of these bags are used each year, consumption of other types of single-use plastic is much higher. In fact, many studies have shown that plastic bags are responsible for a relatively small proportion of the plastic waste currently polluting the planet. Therefore, unless the main sources of plastic waste are regulated, we are unlikely to see any benefits from controlling plastic bag usage. As with any environmental issue, individual responsibility is crucial in the fight against plastic waste.

IELTS Academic Reading

Although plastic bag restrictions have mainly been welcomed by the public, they don't seem to have encouraged people to re-evaluate their consumption habits. Psychologists warn of the risk of "compensatory behaviour", where people believe that one positive step makes up for all their other destructive actions. Since consumers are willing to obey the rules on plastic bag usage, they may feel that they have done enough to protect the environment, and therefore take no further steps to reduce their ecological impact.

Measures on plastic bags can only be effective when taken in conjunction with more far-reaching measures. There needs to be a fundamental shift in the way society thinks, so that we move from wasteful linear systems of industrial production to more circular systems which renew, recycle and re-use resources at every stage.

Questions 15–19
Complete the flow chart below.

Choose **NO MORE THAN TWO WORDS** from the text for each answer.

Write your answers in gaps 15–19.

Linear Economic Systems

A linear economic system approaches **(15)**_____ from a perspective which can be described as "take, make, discard".

↓

(16)_____ are obtained from the earth so that products can be made.

↓

In a linear system, most goods and products are designed to be used just **(17)**_____.

↓

Once the product has been used, it is discarded. In many cases, these items are not **(18)**_____.

↓

Disposing of most products creates environmental harm and leads to huge amounts of **(19)**_____.

Questions 20–23

Choose the correct letter, A, B, C or D.

Write the correct letter **A–G** in answer boxes 20–23.

20　The development of plastic has enabled

　　A　firms to produce goods in high quantities.

　　B　manufacturers to design goods that last longer.

　　C　retailers to discard fewer items.

　　D　firms to reduce their production costs.

21　According to the writer, authorities have focused mainly on plastic bag usage because

　　A　these products cause the most damage to marine areas.

　　B　it is seen as an easy environmental measure to take.

　　C　these products contain some of the highest levels of plastic.

　　D　this measure raises the highest amount of money in taxes.

22　What does the United Nations report reveal?

　　A　Where plastic bag bans have been introduced

　　B　Which countries export the most plastic waste

　　C　How developing countries are affected by plastic waste

　　D　Why countries differ in their approaches to limiting plastic bags

23　According to the text, a plastic bag ban had little effect on people's behaviour in

　　A　India

　　B　California

　　C　The Philippines

　　D　Portugal

IELTS Academic Reading

Questions 24–26
Answer the questions below using **NO MORE THAN THREE WORDS** from the passage for each answer.

Write your answers in boxes 24–26.

24 How many countries have taken measures to limit plastic bag usage?

25 What do many governments invest in with the money they collect from plastic bag taxes?

26 What term is used in the text to mean the belief that positive and harmful actions balance out?

Question 27
Choose the correct letter, A, B, C, D, or E.
Which of the following is the most suitable title for Reading Passage 2?

Write the correct letter **A–E** in the answer box below.

A The impacts of plastic waste on wildlife

B Do consumers actually care about plastic waste?

C How plastic waste mismanagement became a global issue

D Is restricting plastic bags the key to tackling the plastic waste problem?

E Comparing the effectiveness of different plastic bag restrictions

READING PASSAGE 3

You should spend about 20 minutes on Questions 28–40, which are based on Reading Passage 3 below.

Diet and Nutrition

Nutritional science is the branch of science examining how diet affects living organisms. Nutritional scientists investigate the chemical and biological responses that occur during the process of consuming and digesting food. Studying these physiological responses can help scientists to understand more about the relationship between diet and health. This information has played a vital role in shaping public policy for decades. For instance, governments often refer to the latest research findings from nutritional science when making important decisions about food taxation and regulations, and developing public education campaigns about healthy eating. However, recently academic focus has shifted towards a wider range of issues related to diet.

Fascinating research findings suggest that some creatures analyse situations and adjust their behaviour according to dietary needs. In a study conducted by the University of Cambridge, researchers investigated sea creatures called cuttlefish, and how they search for food. They found that when they provided the cuttlefish with a regular and predictable supply of their preferred food source, shrimps, in the evening, the creatures adopted a selective strategy during the day. The cuttlefish ate fewer crabs or other types of food even when they had the opportunity to do so. By contrast, when supplies of food in the evening were unpredictable and irregular, the cuttlefish adopted opportunistic foraging, meaning they took every opportunity to eat during the day.

As for human diets, the link between food and emotions has been an important area of academic focus for several years. Numerous studies have examined the emotional factors driving people to eat unhealthy food or to eat too much. For instance, a study conducted at the National Institute of Health and Welfare in Finland revealed a clear link between emotional stress and a tendency to overeat. Interestingly, the findings suggested so-called "stress eating" is more common among women. The Finnish researchers reported that women were more likely to overeat when they were experiencing stress. Another study at Deakin University in Australia found that when people are subject to significant stress in their life, their food preferences change and they are more likely to eat food that is high in fat or sugar.

Researchers have also examined whether what people eat can actually change the way they feel. For example, various studies, including reports published by Wake Forest University in America, have identified the mood-enhancing qualities of chocolate. Chocolate is thought to lower feelings of anxiety and increase feelings of pleasure or happiness. Furthermore, people's mood can be affected by a lack of particular nutrients in their diet. Researchers at the University of New South Wales in Australia have highlighted how omega-3 fatty acids, found mainly in seafood, affect mood. They found that diets deficient in this nutrient may be linked to several mood disorders, such as depression. Of course, further research is necessary to identify why certain types of food affect how people feel, but the research conducted so far has clearly demonstrated that nutrition plays a role beyond regulating physical health.

As modern lifestyles have changed eating habits across the world, this has raised many interesting questions regarding the impact of so-called "junk food", which is processed food high in fat, sugar and salt. While we have known for a long time that excessive consumption of such food increases the risk of a range of physical conditions including heart disease, diabetes and high blood pressure, the latest studies are now focusing on identifying potential links between junk food consumption and behavioural or cognitive issues. This is a fascinating area of research, and one which could potentially change the message that educators give to the public about the importance of nutrition.

One study which has gained particular attention in the media was undertaken by Macquarie University in Australia in 2020. The study showed that spending just one week eating junk food can impair important cognitive functions in the brain, such as the ability to remember and process information. Participants in this study performed less well on memory tests after eating a diet consisting of nothing but junk food for a week. The participants also reported wanting to eat more of the same, meaning that unhealthy snacks became increasingly appealing to them during the study.

IELTS Academic Reading

What makes the Macquarie study so important is that it proves that junk food can actually alter the brain. It is thought that this type of food disrupts a region in the brain called the hippocampus which plays a major role in our ability to form memories. Crucially, the hippocampus also controls people's appetite. This study shows how people can easily fall into a cycle of eating unhealthy food, which in turn makes them want to eat more. In fact, one of the lead professors behind the Macquarie study has stated that it strengthens the case for junk food to be regulated in a similar way to such addictive products as cigarettes, and he is not alone in this view.

The significance of dietary research should never be underestimated. These studies help scientists, medical practitioners and psychologists to discover more about the specific ways in which diet affects wellbeing. In this way, academic investigation can result in practical applications that can bring long-term, real-world benefits.

Questions 28–34
Complete each idea with the correct research study A–F from the box below.

*Write the correct letter **A–F** in answer boxes 28–34.*

N.B. You may use any letter more than once.

28 The connection between stress and overeating seems to be stronger in females.

29 Stress may affect the types of food people want to eat.

30 Eating chocolate may have a positive effect on mood.

31 Overconsumption of junk food can lead to an increasing appetite for this type of food.

32 Insufficient quantities of certain nutrients can have serious negative impacts on people's mood.

33 Availability of food can influence the decision making or behaviour of some animals.

34 There is a link between the consumption of junk food and poor cognitive performance.

> A Deakin University
> B Cambridge University
> C Wake Forest University
> D National Institute of Health and Welfare
> E University of New South Wales
> F Macquarie University

Test 5

Questions 35–39
Complete the sentences below using **NO MORE THAN THREE WORDS** from the passage for each answer.

Write your answers in boxes 35–39.

35 For many years, research findings from the field of nutritional science have influenced …

36 Cuttlefish eat less during the day if they believe they will later be able to eat …

37 Disorders including depression have been linked to a lack of nutrients called …

38 In one study, excessive junk food consumption was found to negatively affect people's memory after only …

39 As studies suggest people can become addicted to unhealthy food, some people would like it …

Question 40
Choose the correct letter, A, B, C, D, or E.
What is the writer's purpose in Reading Passage 3?
Write the correct letter **A–D** in the answer box below.

A To describe the relationship between diet and intelligence

B To evaluate different approaches to nutritional science research

C To highlight the importance of investigating diet and nutrition

D To argue for improvements in healthy-eating campaigns

IELTS Reading Academic

Test 6

READING PASSAGE 1

You should spend about 20 minutes on **Questions 1–14**, which are based on Reading Passage 1 below.

Culture Shock

The thrill of experiencing new sights, sounds and unfamiliar customs is one of the main attractions for many tourists who travel overseas. Spending time in a foreign culture can be an exciting break from routine, and a chance to have new adventures. And of course, since tourists only spend time in a new culture on a temporary basis, their positive impressions generally last for their entire stay. But what about people who immerse themselves in a foreign culture for a longer period? For instance, globalisation has created more opportunities than ever before to work or study abroad. Such opportunities are certainly appealing, but how do people adjust to a new life overseas?

Moving abroad requires careful planning. For instance, there are practical matters to consider such as finding accommodation and completing all the official paperwork. Then, of course, new arrivals need to figure out how to find their way around their new city, while also getting used to their new job or study programme. With all these issues to take care of, not to mention the emotional stress of moving away from friends and family, it's clear that moving to a foreign country simply cannot be compared with taking a holiday overseas.

Acculturation, or adapting to a different culture, can be extremely challenging. No matter how carefully people try to prepare for their move, there will still be times when they feel overwhelmed in their new country. The intense emotions people feel when adapting to an unfamiliar context are known as "culture shock". The concept was first described by the Canadian academic Kalervo Oberg in the 1950s. Oberg viewed acculturation as a process consisting of different stages during which people may experience a range of emotions. Understanding the acculturation process can help people when they experience difficulties in their host country.

Interestingly, many new arrivals cope remarkably well in the host country at first. People's enthusiasm for their new adventure initially makes up for any confusion they encounter. This is known as the "honeymoon stage", because people view the new culture positively. Although they may experience things that they aren't used to, they regard these experiences as charming or interesting. In fact, it's fair to say that the honeymoon stage gives people unrealistic expectations about the reality of living in a foreign country. But at some point, the initial excitement fades. This is when many people experience culture shock.

During the honeymoon stage, people mistakenly assume that they have successfully completed the transition from one culture to another. Therefore, experiencing culture shock after a few months can be very distressing. What usually follows is a period of frustration, often referred to as the "rejection stage", where they become critical of the host culture. Customs or values they viewed as interesting during the honeymoon stage can become annoying. In particular, people start to feel frustrated that they cannot communicate as well as they can in their own culture, and may feel tired of being perceived as an "outsider". They may experience a range of negative emotions including anger, anxiety and isolation.

People may resent struggling to understand the local way of doing things, and become homesick. They make unfair comparisons to the culture they left behind. They become nostalgic for all the things they miss about their home country, and forget about the negative aspects they used to dislike. At this point, some people may even decide that they cannot adapt to the new culture, and return home. However, socialising with locals, acknowledging that no culture is perfect, and asking for help may reduce this desire. In fact, many companies and universities now offer support programmes to help international employees or students feel less isolated.

The feelings experienced during the rejection stage are completely normal and eventually fade for most people. If they come through this period, people can progress to the "adjustment stage". As the name suggests, the adjustment stage is a period where daily routines become more familiar. While there are still challenging cultural differences, people's ability to cope with them is stronger. Nevertheless, people in this phase may feel like "outsiders" as they haven't had time to develop the strong bonds or relationships that they had in their home countries.

People enter the "adaptation stage" when they feel more or less integrated in the new culture. They can survive and even thrive in their new context. They have learned to appreciate both their native culture and the new one, and they feel comfortable in both. They recognise the flaws and qualities of both cultures, and can navigate life in both contexts. Acculturation shouldn't be viewed as a linear process, because people don't necessarily experience all the stages. It's also common for people to return to an earlier stage temporarily. For instance, people who have generally adjusted may have a sudden period of homesickness. It should also be noted that the acculturation process teaches people to respect both a new culture and aspects of their own culture that they may never have considered before. It also helps people to develop self-reliance and the ability to consider issues from different perspectives.

Questions 1–6
Complete the diagram below.
Choose **NO MORE THAN TWO WORDS** from Reading Passage 1 for each answer.
Do not write articles (a, an, the).

Write your answers in gaps 1–6.

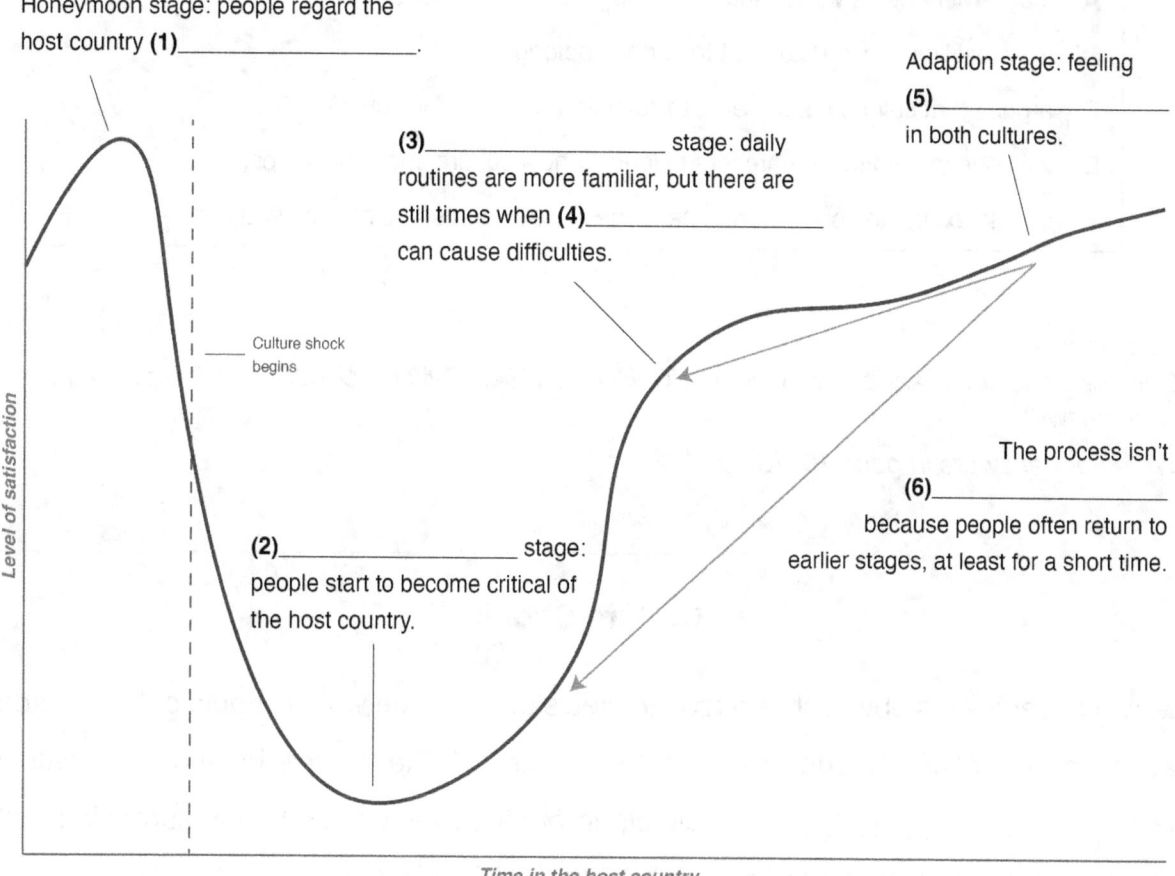

IELTS Academic Reading

Questions 7–9
Complete each sentence with the correct ending A–E from the box below.

Write the correct letter **A–E** in answer boxes 7–9.

N.B. You may use any letter more than once.

7   An academic from Canada

8   When people haven't completely settled into their host country, they

9   Compared with tourists on holiday, people who move abroad to work of study

> A   may experience a wider range of feelings about the host country.
> B   may feel like outsiders or that they don't belong.
> C   argued that culture shock can be prevented with careful planning.
> D   was one of the first researchers to identify how culture shock develops.
> E   should expect to spend more time in the honeymoon stage of acculturation.

Questions 10–13
Complete the summary below. Chose **NO MORE THAN TWO WORDS** from the passage for each answer.

Write your answers in gaps 10–13.

Culture Shock

Moving overseas is obviously a major life decision, and one which should only be made after careful consideration. Nevertheless, with all the professional or education (10)_____ available in other countries, it's hardly surprising that more people are taking advantage of today's globalised world.

Acculturation is the process of adapting to life in an unfamiliar culture. Since (11)_____, it has been known that this process can involve various stages, and people may go through a range of confusing emotions known as "culture shock".

At first, many people find that all the new experiences are interesting and exciting, but this can give them **(12)**_____ of what living in a foreign country is really like.

After this "honeymoon period", many people can feel disappointed when they notice that their host country isn't the perfect place they'd first imagined. This can lead to a difficult time filled with many negative emotions. However, it's important to understand that having such feelings is entirely **(13)**_____. Over time, they are usually replaced with more positive emotions as people become more familiar with their host country.

Question 14
What is the writer's purpose in Reading Passage 1?
Choose the correct letter, A, B, C or D.

Write the correct letter **A–D** in the answer box below.

A   To encourage people to appreciate foreign cultures

B   To suggest ways that people can overcome culture shock

C   To describe typical experiences people have while adjusting to a new culture

D   To argue that living in a foreign country can help people understand their native culture

READING PASSAGE 2

You should spend about 20 minutes on Questions 15–27, which are based on Reading Passage 2 below.

The Houseplant Craze

Section A

Houseplants are fast becoming the trendiest way to add style to our interiors. A beautiful plant in a striking pot can add colour to even the dullest of rooms. From spiky, sculptural cacti to romantic, exotic orchids, the variety of houseplants available to consumers nowadays is astonishing. It's possible to find the ideal plant for any interior, no matter the temperature, amount of sunlight or humidity level of the space. The increasing number of social media influencers focusing on houseplant content highlights how trendy and desirable plants are becoming. But is the current houseplant craze destined to be a passing fad?

Section B

While the cultivation of indoor plants for decorative purposes has a history dating back at least three thousand years, its popularity has risen and fallen throughout the ages. Plants began to be exported around the world in large quantities in the nineteenth century, and since then gardening trends have rarely remained constant. However, fashion alone doesn't seem to account for the sustained surge in popularity that houseplants have had in recent times. For one thing, unlike in previous decades where only particular plant species were in fashion, there's now widespread interest in growing all sorts of plants. What's more, houseplants now seem to appeal to a much wider range of people in society than ever before.

Section C

Globally, the indoor plant market has grown by over 10% and is forecast to reach a value of $726 million within five years. In the UK, companies specialising in indoor plants are reporting a boom in sales, with up to 70% of purchases made by young adults. Garden centres and online plant retailers are reporting significant growth in houseplant sales. It's a similar story in the US, where sales have risen fastest amongst consumers under 35 years old. At the same time, market research indicates that, regardless of age, the number of first-time houseplant buyers is growing. But what is driving this desire for indoor greenery?

Section D

The potential link between increasing urbanisation and the popularity of cultivating indoor plants is difficult to ignore. One major British houseplant supplier recently reported that over two-thirds of all purchases were made by people living in London. As more of us are living in crowded, overpopulated cities with limited access to green spaces, we are bringing nature into our homes instead. At the same time, many people in cities, especially young adults, do not own their own homes. Rental agreements often forbid tenants from having pets or making major interior design changes. Growing houseplants can therefore enable us to put a personal stamp on the places we rent, making them feel cosier and more like our own homes.

Section E

The current houseplant trend might also reflect society's growing realisation that we should appreciate nature more. As public green spaces such as parks, woods and fields are lost due to urban development, people are attempting to preserve nature in whatever way they can. Growing houseplants may seem like an insignificant step, but it is one way we can stay connected with the natural world. Houseplants represent the world beyond our electronics, high-rise buildings and air pollution. They remind us of the green places the world is at risk of losing.

Section F

In fact, some indoor gardeners are convinced that houseplants can actually improve air quality. This belief mainly stems from experiments conducted in 1989 by NASA scientists investigating whether plants could be used to filter toxic chemicals on space stations. The plants in the study removed over 70 per cent of the chemicals in the air within 24 hours. But, unfortunately, this research has limited practical applications on Earth. The NASA study was conducted under very controlled conditions that reflected the unique conditions found in space. Subsequent studies have shown that plants have virtually no effect on air quality in real homes. An extremely high quantity of plants would be needed to produce even minimal air-quality benefits.

Section G
Nevertheless, people may gain mental and psychological benefits from plants. The therapeutic effects of exposure to nature have been known for a long time, and studies indicate that even indoor plants may have a beneficial influence on people's stress levels, productivity and even their ability to concentrate. In hospitals, some research suggests that plants may play a role in reducing patients' pain levels after surgery. Although these studies should be interpreted with caution, it's clear that plants do more than simply look pretty. With this in mind, it's hardly surprising that they are now a common sight in many workplaces, as well as in private homes.

Section H
From yoga to alternative therapies, the booming "wellness" industry highlights how people are placing more emphasis on their physical and mental wellbeing than ever before. Indoor gardening may be an extension of this. While we should challenge the most extreme claims about what can be achieved by filling our homes with plants, any trend that encourages people to appreciate nature should be applauded!

Questions 15–19
Reading Passage 2 has 8 sections labelled A–H.
Which paragraph contains the following information?

Write the correct letter **A–H** in answer boxes 15–19.

NB: You may use any letter more than once.

15 evidence that claims about the environmental benefits of houseplants are misleading

16 a reason why people who rent their homes may like houseplants

17 a suggestion that the current popularity of houseplants is unlike earlier houseplant trends

18 commercial evidence of the increasing popularity of houseplants

19 a reason why houseplants are popular in places where people work

IELTS Academic Reading

Questions 20–23
Do the following statements agree with the claims of the writer in Reading Passage 2?
In boxes 20–23, write:

TRUE   If the statement agrees with the information in the passage
FALSE   If the statement contradicts the information in the passage
NOT GIVEN   If there is no information on this in the passage

20   The amount of information relating to houseplants is growing on social media.

21   The practice of growing plants inside began in the nineteenth century.

22   Houseplant sales have overtaken sales of other gardening products in the US.

23   Indoor plants have been found to help people stay focused.

Questions 24–27
Complete the sentences below using **NO MORE THAN THREE WORDS** from the passage for each answer.

Write your answers in boxes 24–27.

24   One of the main houseplant retailers in the UK sells the majority of its houseplants to customers …

25   Growing houseplants in urban homes can be seen as way for people to try to …

26   The NASA study led to a popular belief that houseplants have the ability to …

27   Some studies have suggested that plants could be used in medical contexts to decrease people's …

READING PASSAGE 3

You should spend about 20 minutes on Questions 28–40, which are based on Reading Passage 3 below.

Perfectly Imperfect?

Charlotte Morris reflects on a craft like no other

Section A

I've always been artistic, but over the years my creative passions have evolved. I used to enjoy arts and crafts that I could use in my everyday life. And, while I'm still interested in activities like photography, dressmaking and cake decoration, in recent times my creativity has taken me in new directions. I've become more focused on exploring artistic pursuits simply for the joy of creating something beautiful. I'm especially keen on artforms that require attention to detail and precision. For instance, I get a lot of satisfaction from perfecting the delicate patterns of calligraphy, or trying to master oil painting brushstroke techniques. In that sense, I suppose I might be described as a "perfectionist". I don't stop practising until I create a piece of art that I consider to be completely free of fault.

Section B

One of my newest passions is ceramics. In many ways, it's the ideal pastime for me. The art of creating beautiful, decorative vases, dishes or plates requires a lot of skill but also results in wonderful objects I can enjoy and use at home. I've taken quite a few courses in recent years, and it's been interesting to discover more about the different ceramic styles found around the world. My skills continue to improve, and I'm very proud of some of the pieces I've created. In fact, my friends now beg me to make objects for them, which gives me enormous pleasure!

Section C

When a colleague suggested that I should give the Japanese art of *kintsugi* a try, I was intrigued. Having never heard of it before, the first thing I did was search for kintsugi images online to understand more about what it was, or what it looked like. The search engine displayed a series of images of beautiful ceramics decorated with delicate, gold lines. It also showed textiles and clothing with "kintsugi prints", all decorated with similarly fine lines. Because of this, I assumed that the word kintsugi referred to making eye-catching designs using straight lines arranged in random patterns. I was wrong about that and many other things!

Section D

I was surprised to discover that kintsugi is actually about repairing objects rather than making them. It's the practice of repairing a ceramic object by sticking all the broken pieces back together again. What makes kintsugi items look so distinctive is the glue used to stick the broken pieces together. The glue, or lacquer, contains precious metals in powder form, such as silver, platinum or, more usually, gold. In fact, the word kintsugi can be translated as "to join or mend with gold". Those beautiful golden lines that had caught my eye online are actually where broken pieces have been stuck back together. As the number and position of the broken pieces determine where the golden lacquer lines are placed, each repaired object has a completely unique appearance.

Section E

Keen to understand more, I joined a workshop to learn about different types of kintsugi repair. I learned that the gold lines I'd seen online are known as the "crack" style. But this method isn't possible when some of the pieces of a broken object are missing. In this case, the "piece method" can be used, because the gaps are filled with the lacquer, creating golden shapes on the object. Perhaps the most unusual repair style is the "joint call". In this approach, missing pieces are replaced with ceramic fragments from another object. As a result, the repaired piece ends up with different patterns, colours or styles. The teacher's enthusiasm for kintsugi brought the class to life, but the highlight was having the chance to try the different techniques myself. That's when I realised how much skill and patience is required to complete the repairs!

Section F

Although gaining a new artistic skill was my main motivation for signing up for the workshop, I learned far more than that. It definitely challenged the way I value objects. As someone who has always regarded damaged objects as less valuable, I found it fascinating to see how kintsugi actually celebrates the flaws in objects. Rather than attempting to repair a broken object by returning it to its original condition, kintsugi actually highlights the breaks, and turns these "imperfections" into something beautiful and unique. In fact, the workshop teacher explained that kintsugi repairs have become so valued that, nowadays, brand-new ceramics are actually produced to look as if they have been repaired!

IELTS Academic Reading

Section G
The more I learned about this wonderful craft, the more I realised that its principles can be applied in everyday life. Kintsugi turns negatives into positives, and celebrates "imperfections" as signs of experience and growth. It made me realise that society is too often focused on making everything perfect, and that, because of this, we sometimes miss the beauty of life. By contrast, kintsugi encourages us to appreciate what we have, like celebrating the lines on our face as signs of our growing wisdom, or the scars on our skin as signs of our strength. No other hobby has ever taught me such a valuable life lesson!

Questions 28–33
Reading Passage 3 has 7 sections, A–G.
Choose the correct headings for Sections **A–B** and **D–G** from the list of headings below.
Write the correct number i–viii in answer boxes 28–33.

List of headings

i	Making pottery	v	Why kintsugi has become so popular
ii	First impressions of an unfamiliar craft	vi	A love of creativity
iii	Understanding kintsugi	vii	A new perspective on objects
iv	A positive approach to life	viii	Learning about forms of kintsugi

Example:

Section C — Answer: ii

28 Section A
29 Section B
30 Section D
31 Section E
32 Section F
33 Section G

Test 6

Questions 34–37
Answer the questions below using **NO MORE THAN THREE WORDS** from the passage for each answer.

Write your answers in boxes 34–37.

34 Which creative activity has the writer focused on in recent years?

35 Who recommended that the writer learn about kintsugi?

36 Which metal is most commonly found in kintsugi lacquer?

37 Which method can only be used when all the broken pieces of an object are available?

Questions 38–40
Choose the correct letter, A, B, C or D.

Write the correct letter **A–D** in answer boxes 38–40.

38 Which of the following best describes the writer's attitude to her hobbies before learning about kintsugi?

   A   Mistakes lead to learning.
   B   Practice makes perfect.
   C   Art should be shared.
   D   Creativity should have a practical purpose.

39 The writer initially thought kintsugi involved

   A   designing clothes inspired by Japanese culture.
   B   using gold to decorate objects.
   C   creating patterns using lines.
   D   printing patterns directly onto objects.

40 The writer originally decided to take the kintsugi course because she wanted to

    A add a new technique to her creative skills.

    B create the objects she had seen online.

    C have the chance to learn from expert teachers.

    D put the skills she had been studying into practice.

IELTS Reading Academic

Test 7

IELTS Academic Reading

READING PASSAGE 1

You should spend about 20 minutes on Questions 1–14, which are based on Reading Passage 1 below.

In some European countries, sales of animal-based dairy milk have halved since the mid-1970s, and similar trends have been reported in the US. By contrast, interest in milk products derived from plant sources such as soya beans, rice, or nuts has exploded in recent years. The plant-milk sector has annual growth of 20%, and the market is now estimated to be worth at least $2.5 billion. The plant-milk market is dominated by almond milk, which accounts for 68% of all plant-milk sales, and is the most well-known plant-based alternative to dairy milk.

Plant-milk products were once considered highly specialist items, but they are fast becoming a common sight in supermarkets and cafés. In fact, the range of products available nowadays can be quite overwhelming. Consumers can choose between numerous, different types of plant milk, many of which are offered in sweet and plain versions. Consumers hoping to make the switch away from animal-based products have to compare the individual pros and cons of different options to find the product that meets their specific needs.

Many consumers are becoming increasingly uncomfortable with the ethics of consuming animal products. Such concerns have led to a growing number of people excluding all animal products from their diets. Obviously, since all plant milks are animal-free, these consumers can simply select a plant milk based on taste or cost. Their choice may also depend on how they plan to use the milk. For instance, some products such as rice milk are less suitable for cooking compared to products made from nuts or soya.

However, when consumer choices are influenced by factors beyond basic taste preferences or financial considerations, selecting the right plant milk becomes far more difficult. For instance, many people are interested in plant milk because these products are believed to be heathier than dairy milk. However, making comparisons between different types of milk is highly complex since every product comes with health-related pros and cons.

It is known that cow's milk has higher amounts of saturated fat than plant-based alternatives. Diets high in saturated fat can lead to serious medical problems including heart disease. Dairy milk also contains more calories than many types of plant milk, which is a consideration for people concerned about weight management. A cup of cow's milk contains, on average, 152 calories, whereas almond milk contains just 40 calories per cup. However, not all plant milks are low in calories. Rice milk, for instance, contains 120 calories per cup, making it almost as calorific as dairy milk.

Of course, milk is an important product for other nutritional reasons. It is a rich source of protein, a nutrient which is vital for healthy muscle development. Dairy milk contains more protein than other types of milk, but plant milk can still be a useful source of protein for people who are avoiding animal products. Milk derived from beans or nuts is a better source of protein than that derived from grains such as oats. In fact, soya milk provides almost as much protein as cow's milk, and almond milk is another reasonable source which fulfils most people's protein requirements.

Comparing different types of milk becomes even harder when analysing the environmental impact. Environmentalists have certainly been concerned about the detrimental effects of animal-based farming for several years. This type of agriculture requires a considerable amount of land. In fact, it has been estimated that producing just one glass of dairy milk requires approximately 650m^2 of land. Cows also release additional CO_2 (greenhouse gases) into the atmosphere, which is known to contribute to global warming. Cows' waste can also pollute the surrounding land or water supplies. Therefore, it is widely accepted that there is a need for more sustainable alternatives.

In terms of carbon emissions, there is a strong argument that all forms of plant milk are better choices for the planet. One recent study showed that plant-milk production creates approximately three times fewer carbon emissions than dairy milk production. And, generally speaking, plant-milk production requires nine times less land. These are two important factors which underline why plant milk has become known for its sustainable image amongst consumers.

However, plant milk is not without its drawbacks. The main problem is that most of the crops used for plant milk require extremely high quantities of water to grow. This is particularly true for rice and almonds. Producing milk from these crops consumes far more water than is used in dairy-milk production.

As demand for plant milk increases, the environmental impacts are becoming clearer. To grow large quantities of crops all year round, farmers often use additional lighting and heating sources, leading to extremely high energy usage. They may also use pesticides which can be harmful for the soil and pollute water supplies. In addition, large-scale almond cultivation is known to have adverse effects on wildlife, especially local bees. As well as the issues associated with pesticide use, almond farming disrupts bees' natural cycles since they are forced to pollinate the trees more often.

Of course, selecting the right milk product is ultimately a matter of personal preference. Whether or not the deciding factor is dietary, environmental or simple taste preferences, there's no doubt that consumers now have more choice than ever before.

Questions 1–6
Complete the table below.
Choose **NO MORE THAN TWO WORDS** from Reading Passage 1 for each answer.
Write your answers in gaps 1–6.

Type of milk	General comments	Nutrition	Environmental impact
Dairy (milk from animal sources)	Demand for products in this sector has been falling	Known to be high in (1)_____ fat	Responsible for high levels of greenhouse gases This type of farming requires the most (2)_____
Rice milk	Not a good choice if the milk will be used for (3)_____ purposes	One cup has on average (4)_____ calories	High water consumption
(5)_____ milk	The market leader in the plant-milk sector	Provides adequate protein for most people's needs	Harmful for (6)_____ populations (e.g. pesticides and disrupts their natural cycles)

IELTS Academic Reading

Questions 7–11
Do the following statements agree with the claims of the writer in Reading Passage 1?
In boxes 7–11, write:

TRUE If the statement agrees with the information in the passage
FALSE If the statement contradicts the information in the passage
NOT GIVEN If there is no information on this in the passage

7   Almond milk is the market leader in the plant-milk sector.

8   Plain plant milk has become more common than sweet plant-milk products.

9   Almond milk has fewer calories than rice milk.

10 Milk from nuts or beans contains more protein than dairy milk.

11 Plant-milk production uses eight times less land than dairy-milk production.

Questions 12–13
Answer the questions below using **NO MORE THAN THREE WORDS** from the passage for each answer.

Write your answers in boxes 12–13.

12 By how much has the plant-milk sector increased?

13 What are extra energy sources used for in large-scale crop agriculture?

Question 14

Which of the following is the most suitable title for Reading Passage 1?
Choose the correct letter, A, B, C, D or E.

Write the correct letter **A–D** in the answer box below.

A   Why plant milk is less eco-friendly than consumers believe

B   How consumers choose between plant and dairy milk

C   Why the plant-milk industry has become so influential

D   How milk trends affect dairy and plant farmers

E   Why the dairy industry is in decline

READING PASSAGE 2

You should spend about 20 minutes on Questions 15–27, which are based on Reading Passage 2 below.

Start-up Success

Laura Willetts shares her business secrets

Section A
Don't let false assumptions about entrepreneurs prevent you from following your start-up ambitions. If your idea of an entrepreneur is a middle-aged business professional in a smart suit, think again. Not all entrepreneurs spend years in the business world before starting their company. While it's certainly not unusual for employees to become business owners after gaining work experience, it's not the only route to start-up success. It's also time we stopped believing that entrepreneurs have to be born with a natural instinct for business. In reality, there's no magic ingredient that ensures success in business; it's about hard work and making smart choices.

Section B
Owning a business can be financially rewarding, but if that's your main motivation, think carefully about whether the risks are worth it. Many employees in senior positions in large companies earn far higher salaries, and of course, have greater financial security. On the other hand, entrepreneurship has many other appealing aspects. I personally get a great deal of satisfaction from turning my creative ideas into business reality. Interestingly, one recent survey showed that this and the chance to be one's own boss were the two main reasons why people wanted to start their own business. This survey revealed that another top priority was the chance to create something for the local community.

Section C

Whatever your reason for setting up a business, you should start with a clear idea. Entrepreneurs spot gaps in the market by identifying a problem which needs to be solved, and developing solutions. However, business ideas don't have to be completely brand-new innovations. Instead, you can improve what is already currently available or find a way to do it in a unique or different way. For instance, many successful business owners identify ways to adapt existing ideas so that they appeal to a different type of consumer. Being an entrepreneur is about noticing these opportunities and finding ways to make them attractive to potential customers.

Section D

Take your time in the initial planning stages of your start-up. Careful preparation can help you to avoid making time-consuming or costly mistakes in the long run. Market research is a key part of this process because it's important to understand your target consumers. Market research can also reveal unexpected problems with your product, or reasons why you might need to change your business plan. One common market-research method is focus groups. This is where a wide variety of consumers share their feedback about your product or service, and it can be an effective way of discovering what the public really thinks.

Section E

You also need to plan how you will cover the costs of starting your business. Unless you have substantial savings, you'll need financial support from external sources. Traditionally, this meant either applying for bank loans or selling a share of your business to investors. More recently, crowdfunding has become a popular funding strategy. Rather than relying on one investor, crowdfunding provides entrepreneurs with numerous investors, all of whom invest relatively small amounts. From the investor's perspective, this reduces the risk since they're not lending large sums. From the entrepreneur's perspective, it means that they don't have to give up so much control of their company. But, of course, whatever decisions you make about funding your start-up, take advantage of professional finance advice.

Section F

In fact, I'd recommend getting as much guidance as possible when starting out. Many young people now study business degrees specifically to learn all about entrepreneurship, and there's certainly value in that. However, if you don't have formal qualifications, don't let a lack of academic training hold you back. As well as all the useful resources available online, it's worth attending local business events and workshops. These events can teach you practical skills, and also offer opportunities to make valuable business connections. They are a great way to gain insights from other entrepreneurs.

Section G

I've learned the hard way that even if you want to have complete control over your business, it's not a smart use of your time. When I first started out, I thought I could handle all the decisions that needed to be made, and I was desperate to be involved in every single activity. Consequently, I wasted a lot of time doing things that I wasn't particularly good at. I now recognise the importance of building the right team around you. You have to accept that others may be more qualified to take on certain roles, so be open to their suggestions. This enables you to spend your time focusing on developing the overall business.

Section H

Of course, no matter how much you prepare, you're bound to make mistakes. It's impossible to avoid all difficulties, but successful entrepreneurs manage to learn from them. When something goes wrong, it provides an opportunity for further growth and a chance to come back even stronger. That's why I think the real key to business is your mindset. If you have the determination and the right attitude, you can turn setbacks into successes.

Questions 15–21
Reading Passage 2 has 8 sections, A–H.
Choose the correct headings for Sections **A–E** and **G–H** from the list of headings below.
Write the correct number i–ix in answer boxes 15–21.

Example:

	Answer
Section F	v

List of headings

i   Why you can't do everything
ii Separating myth from reality
iii Understanding your consumers
iv Learning from failure
v   Benefitting from support
vi Finding inspiration
vii Funding your start-up
viii The financial risks entrepreneurs face
ix What drives entrepreneurs?

15 Section A
16 Section B
17 Section C
18 Section D
19 Section E
20 Section G
21 Section H

IELTS Academic Reading

Questions 22–24
Chose **THREE** letters, A–F. Write the correct letter A–F in answer boxes 22–24.

The list below gives some reasons why people may want to start their own business. Which **THREE** of these reasons are mentioned in the text as the most influential ones according to research?

- **A** The process of turning a concept into something real gives people a sense of achievement.

- **B** Running your own business can bring considerable financial benefits.

- **C** Being an entrepreneur means you have control over your work.

- **D** People enjoy the challenge of doing something which involves risks.

- **E** Setting up a business can provide opportunities to help others.

- **F** You can learn more by running a business than by working for a company.

22
23
24

Questions 25–27
Complete the sentences below using **NO MORE THAN TWO WORDS** from the passage for each answer.

Write your answers in boxes 25–27.

25 In the early stages of a start-up, it's important to understand your customers by conducting …

26 Crowdfunding is thought to be a safer form of investment because individuals don't have to invest …

27 Interest in entrepreneurship can be seen from the growing number of students taking …

READING PASSAGE 3

You should spend about 20 minutes on Questions 28–40, which are based on Reading Passage 3 below.

Skateboarding Cities

Section A
Unlike other popular outdoor pursuits such as football or cycling, skateboarding has had quite a negative reputation throughout its relatively short history, as shown by the lack of government support for it in many places. Sadly, this creative sport has sometimes been misunderstood as something that encourages antisocial behaviour when it actually has a lot to offer youngsters and urban communities. However, there are positive signs that city planners are finally starting to realise the benefits of skateboarding as a way of encouraging people to stay active. Cities are changing their approach to skatepark design. This is an important step because, when skateboarding facilities are planned effectively, they can bring communities together and enhance the urban environment.

Section B
Is there an activity better suited to urban environments than skateboarding? For street skaters, the entire city becomes a playground, where pavements, benches, walls and steps can be used to perform tricks. However, the growing popularity of skateboarding amongst teenagers hasn't always been supported by city authorities. Skateboarding has often been treated as a nuisance that should be contained and restricted rather than as a sport that should be encouraged. As a result, many of the original twentieth-century public skateparks were designed primarily to keep skateboarders out of city centres and off the streets.

Section C
Skateparks became popular in the 1970s, especially in North America. Like tennis courts or swimming pools, skateparks provide people with areas to practise their skills. Skateparks usually include concrete ramps, steps, slopes and metal rails. However, in many cases, public skateparks that were built in the 1970s were unsuitable for skateboarding in cold or wet weather, and had no lighting. These sites were not always maintained well, so over time they fell into such poor condition that they were not safe to use. Additionally, many of them were located in inconvenient locations or in undesirable parts of the city. As skaters found more suitable places instead, skateparks started to attract people behaving in antisocial ways. This, unfairly, created further negative impressions of skateboarding and skaters. Eventually, many of these skateparks were either redeveloped for other purposes or abandoned as "areas to avoid". This shows how poor urban design can isolate and even create tensions between communities.

Section D
Fortunately, there are shining examples around the world of superior ways to serve skaters' needs. Some approaches focus on integrating skateboarding facilities into cities rather than attempt to create separate skating areas. For instance, the local council in the English city of Bristol decided to improve a pedestrian subway area to make it more welcoming for skaters. They improved the surfaces and made the open central area even better for skateboarding by installing a simple low wall at very low cost. These simple changes have transformed the area, making it safer for both skaters and pedestrians.

Section E
In fact, bringing skaters and non-skaters closer together to share the same space can improve cooperation and understanding. Barcelona is known as one of Europe's most "skateboard-friendly" cities. Skateboarding is a common sight throughout this beautiful coastal city, and it is increasingly part of Barcelona's culture. Skateboarding is encouraged and there are numerous areas where the walkways, steps and ledges accommodate skaters' needs without impacting non-skaters. As a result, skaters and non-skaters respect each other. Interestingly, Barcelona has gained a worldwide reputation for skateboarding, and has profited from increased tourism as a result. Local skaters also benefit from the chance to improve their techniques with skaters from all over the world.

Section F
Of course, there is still a need for public skateparks. When skateboarding experts' voices are heard, councils can create facilities suitable for skaters of different levels of skill or experience. Skateparks must be located in safe, popular public areas that have other amenities such as cafés or good transport links. This will encourage more

IELTS Academic Reading

young people to take up the sport and there will be more people around to ensure that they learn how to skate safely, making injuries less likely. It will also make skateboarding a popular leisure option for families, which will open up new commercial and social opportunities in the local area.

Section G
Traditionally, parks and playgrounds have been the main leisure spaces in cities, and there's no doubt that these amenities bring communities together. Skateboarding facilities can offer similar benefits to urban communities, and, in many cases, breathe new life into cities. There's no reason why skateparks can't become part of the urban landscape. However, this can only be achieved if representatives of the skateboarding community are consulted so that the facilities are created in the right way.

Section H
International stars such as Tony Hawks and Sky Brown are inspiring new generations to pick up a skateboard, and it is great to see how they are raising the profile of the sport. Skateboarding teaches people a range of physical skills, and encourages people to overcome challenges. Team spirit is strong within skater communities, and this teaches children about the value of helping one another. Now it is time for cities to create the right environment to enable the sport to develop even further. If they do this, we can all benefit.

Questions 28–33
Reading Passage 3 has 8 sections labelled A–H.
Which paragraph contains the following information?

Write the correct letter **A–H** in answer boxes 28–33.

NB: You may use any letter more than once.

28 An example of how a city has benefitted financially from skateboarding

29 A suggestion about how to make skateparks better for beginners

30 A reason why skateboarding is becoming more popular

31 An inexpensive way to create skateboarding opportunities in cities

32 A definition of the function of skateparks

33 A reason why skaters stopped using many public skateparks

Questions 34–36
Choose the correct letter, A, B, C or D.

*Write the correct letter **A–D** in answer boxes 34–36.*

34 The writer argues that skateboarding should

    A receive more funding than other leisure activities.

    B be applauded for the way it has improved its reputation.

    C be promoted in both urban and rural areas.

    D receive more recognition for the positive influence it can have.

35 What point does the writer make about skateparks from the 1970s?

    A It was a mistake to base them on other sport facilities.

    B Their design flaws eventually had a negative impact on cities.

    C The materials they were made of were difficult to repair.

    D They were built in areas that were too crowded.

36 Barcelona's approach to skateboarding has been to

    A support skateboarding as part of the city's identity.

    B invest tourist revenue in skateboarding facilities.

    C attempt to keep skateboarding away from city centres.

    D focus on developing skateboarding as an international sport.

Questions 37–40
*Complete the summary below. Chose **NO MORE THAN TWO WORDS** from the passage for each answer.*

Write your answers in gaps 37–40.

Skateboarding

As an activity which is closely associated with urban life, skateboarding is a pastime which attracts both positive and negative opinions. For city councils, the challenge is to find ways to encourage people to practise their sport without it becoming a **(37)**_____ to other city residents.

One strategy is **(38)**_____ skateboarding facilities into city streets and neighbourhoods. The benefit of this approach is that skaters and non-skaters learn to respect each other.

Sadly, many skateparks in the past were not designed well. They were not suitable for skating in certain types of **(39)**_____, and were often difficult to reach.

If authorities want to take advantage of what skateboarding can offer, they must design new skateboarding facilities with skaters' needs in mind. In order to do this, it is essential that people who truly understand skateboarding **(40)**_____. This will ensure that the skateparks can benefit both skaters and the local community.

IELTS Reading Academic

Test 8

IELTS Academic Reading

READING PASSAGE 1

You should spend about 20 minutes on Questions 1–14, which are based on Reading Passage 1 below.

The Commercialisation of Sport

The organisers of the London 2012 Olympic Games adopted the slogan "Inspire a generation" with good reason. Elite sport can certainly be a powerful influence on society. Many youngsters are inspired to take up sports after watching incredible athletic feats on TV or at live sporting events. Sports fans daydream about what it would be like to be a professional athlete competing at the very highest level. Even those with limited interest in sport are likely to recognise leading sports stars due to the considerable media attention these individuals receive. The profile of professional sport has never been so high.

We are now in an entirely new era of sports commercialisation. The size of the sports market is incredible. In the US alone, the sports industry is forecasted to be worth over $83 billion within a few years. To put that in context, America's car industry is worth $82 billion, while film and music are worth just under $20 billion combined. Worldwide, the sports market is expected to reach almost $600 billion within a decade. Perhaps an even clearer sign of sport's growing status is the creation of brand-new employment opportunities. Professional sport now involves roles such as sports agents, sports statisticians and sports lawyers. This has also led to degree courses designed to help students to develop careers in the professional sports sector.

Since 1945, sport has increasingly become a commodity to be exploited for commercial gain. The term "golden triangle" is used to explain how this commercialisation of sport has developed. The golden triangle consists of three core elements, which are the sport itself, media and corporate sponsors. These three elements depend heavily on one another for consumers and revenue. Without this golden triangle, sport wouldn't occupy such a prominent role in modern society.

Naturally, the more popular a sport is, the more value it has to broadcasters and, therefore, sponsors. Broadcasters are willing to pay more for the rights to popular sports. This in turn helps the sport to develop further because the money received from broadcasting can be invested in improving facilities and coaching, and attracting top international athletes. It also gives the sport a bigger platform through which even more fans can be reached. From the media's perspective, the more the sport grows the bigger audiences it will attract, which enables broadcasters and media outlets to increase their own advertising revenues.

Despite the considerable financial benefits, there are concerns about whether media outlets now interfere too much in professional sport. For instance, broadcasters can control when matches are held so that they can maximise their audience ratings, even if this is not in the best interests of the athletes or fans attending the events. Athletes are also required to take part in press conferences and interviews for the media, which can be a hugely stressful distraction. Also, since the media focuses on the most popular sports, the financial gap between mainstream and minority sports is widening. This means that less well-known sports struggle to gain attention or interest. If these sports receive no media coverage, how will they inspire the next generation to take them up?

The third component of the golden triangle, corporate sponsorship, has also been criticised. Companies pay considerable sums to sports broadcasters for the right to sponsor their coverage, and also for advertising time during commercial breaks. Sponsorship is also a vital source of funding for major sports competitions and events. There's no doubt that global tournaments such as the football World Cup or Olympic Games rely heavily on corporate investment. This means that events find it difficult to refuse funding from companies, and, as a result, may become associated with products or brands that conflict with the core principles of the sport. For instance, is it really acceptable for sporting events to take sponsorship from fast-food companies? Surely it would be better to sacrifice some financial support to send the right message to audiences.

Companies also pay to sponsor sports teams or individual athletes. Naturally, the most successful athletes and clubs receive the best sponsorship deals because companies aim to gain as much attention as possible. This increases the gap between big and small teams competing in the same sport, which can give bigger clubs an unfair competitive advantage. In the case of individual sponsorship deals, athletes are expected to represent a particular image at all times for their sponsors, even in their free time. This puts additional pressure on them because if they don't behave exactly how the company wants at all times, they may lose their sponsorship deals.

Commercial interests are transforming professional sport. It is often argued that, since sport has gained so much media coverage and corporate promotion, athletic standards have improved. This is certainly valid since competing at an elite level requires significant financial resources. Sports may be reaching new audiences, which is definitely a positive if it encourages more people to be active. However, there is also a risk that the true meaning of sport is being sacrificed in the pursuit of financial rewards.

Questions 1–5
Look at the following criticisms and the features of modern sport below.
Match each criticism with the correct feature, A–D from the box below.

Write the correct letter **A–D** in answer boxes 1–5.

N.B. You may use any letter more than once.

1 There is a temptation to accept investment from unsuitable sources.

2 It means athletes have less control over their lives.

3 Sports decisions are made without considering the needs of fans or competitors.

4 It can lead to inequality within sports competitions.

5 Less popular sports are negatively affected.

A	Sponsorship of individual athletes
B	Sports broadcasting
C	Corporate sponsorship of clubs and teams
D	Corporate sponsorship of sports events

Questions 6–10
Do the following statements agree with the claims of the writer in Reading Passage 1?

In boxes 6–10, write:

YES   If the statement agrees with the claims of the writer
NO   If the statement contradicts the claims of the writer
NOT GIVEN   If it is impossible to say what the writer thinks about this

6 Careers in sport have become more in demand than careers in music and film.

7 The cost of live sport coverage differs based on which channel is showing the event.

8 Less well-known athletes find media duties more stressful than elite sports stars do.

IELTS Academic Reading

9 Financial backing should be refused if there is a potential conflict with the values of an event.

10 Commercialisation may improve the quality of sports performance.

Questions 11–14
Complete the summary using the list of words or phrases, A–I, below.
Write the correct letter, **A–I**, in boxes 11–14.

The Golden Triangle

Professional sport is a product that can be bought and sold like any other good or service. The commercialisation of sport has developed through the interaction of three main (11)_____.

The (12)_____ sport receives from broadcasting rights can be used to develop its facilities or recruit trainers or athletes. Companies also contribute to the commercialisation of sport by sponsoring events or individual athletes.

There's no doubt that the golden triangle has raised the profile of sport, but it raises questions about the integrity of sport too. Commercial considerations should not (13)_____ how sports events are organised or run. Also, commercialisation tends to favour the most popular teams. This makes it even harder for smaller teams to compete on an equal (14)_____. This surely goes against the fundamental principle of competitive sport.

A	markets	B	income	C	determine
D	standard	E	sales	F	aspects
G	elite	H	prevent	I	basis

Test 8

READING PASSAGE 2

You should spend about 20 minutes on Questions 15–27, which are based on Reading Passage 2 below.

School Schedules

Section A

In many countries, the academic calendar has been in place for decades. The same applies for the timing and duration of the school day. Many of these school timetables were set long before research first began to be conducted on how students learn best. Therefore, it's unlikely that these schedules were originally created with specific educational purposes in mind. This has prompted educational experts to suggest that the time has come for schools to consider whether their schedules really meet students' learning needs. In particular, there are growing calls for the school day itself to be revised for teenage students.

Section B

During adolescence, people's natural sleep/wake rhythms change, meaning that there is a shift in the times when people feel sleepy or alert. Numerous studies have shown that teenagers don't feel sleepy until around 11pm. Even if they go to bed earlier than this, they will naturally find it difficult to fall asleep. At the same time, significant physical and cognitive changes occur during adolescence. Consequently, teenagers require on average one hour more sleep than they did during childhood. Given these two factors, it's hardly surprising that, around the world, many teenagers suffer from the effects of insufficient sleep if they must get up early for school.

Section C

It's highly likely that, when the school day begins before 10am, teenagers are too tired to focus on their lessons effectively. Over the long term, this has been shown to negatively affect teenagers' academic achievement. Sleep loss is also known to interfere with people's physical health. For instance, when people do not get adequate sleep, the body produces hormones that increases their appetite for food containing high amounts of fat, salt or sugar. Sleep loss has also been linked to mental-health issues including depression. Given all these issues, the case for starting the school day later is hard to ignore. If we have the possibility of improving school for students, is there any valid reason to retain the same school schedules that have been in place for decades?

Section D

Some schools have already started experimenting with changes to the school day, and there are convincing signs that later starts are bringing positive outcomes. One practical benefit has been that more students have time in the morning to have a decent, nutritious breakfast. As for academic impacts, in a three-year study in the US, pupils' class grades and national test results improved when later school start times were introduced. Similar results were reported in a study conducted in the UK. Moving to later start times resulted in significant improvements in academic performances amongst teenage pupils, and there were fewer cases of illness-related absences as well. Research in countries including Australia, Sweden and Singapore also confirms these findings: the clear message is that adjusting the school day to fits teenagers' natural sleep patterns supports learning.

Section E

Even so, changing the school day has obvious practical implications that have to be considered. Delaying the start of school will make it impossible for working parents to take their children to school. And any change to the start of the school day naturally affects the finish time as well. In some Northern Hemisphere countries, children could end up travelling home in the dark during winter. Later finishing times may also mean less time for after-school activities such as drama clubs or school sports. These activities are important for students' social development. There is also the concern that students won't have enough time to complete all their homework or studies if the school day finishes later. These valid practical concerns explain why many authorities remain reluctant to introduce radical changes to school schedules.

Section F

Opponents argue that schedule changes will disrupt teenagers' night-time routine. The fear is that it will encourage them to go to bed later. For instance, teenagers might be tempted to stay up playing video games if school starts later. However, this idea is hard to defend. Teenagers' natural biological clocks will let them know when it is time to go to bed. The later school start will simply enable them to get sufficient sleep. Nevertheless, the broader point about night-time routines is an important one, because parents have a role to play in this. Research has shown that using electronic devices in the evening can interfere with people's natural sleep patterns. Therefore, teenagers' screen time should be restricted before going to bed. Parents have a responsibility to help teenagers make smart choices in the evening.

Section G

There is overwhelming evidence that later school times can lead to more productive lessons and healthier, happier students. However, one worrying idea that has been suggested is for schools to fit more time into the school day by removing breaks and lunchtime. Although this may enable schools to "catch up" on a later start without finishing the school day much later, it is certainly not the right policy. It should be obvious that people cannot learn effectively without breaks, and pupils definitely need lunch if we want them to stay focused in the afternoon. Therefore, schools, parents and local authorities need to work together to create a school schedule that works on both practical and educational levels.

Questions 15–20
Reading Passage 2 has 7 sections, A–G.
Choose the correct headings for Sections **A–F** from the list of headings below.

Write the correct number i–viii in answer boxes 15–20.

List of headings

i   The teenage body clock
ii Implementing the right changes
iii Potential disadvantages of school schedule changes
iv Studies on the role of sleep in learning
v   Established school routines
vi Evidence for changing the school schedule
vii How lack of sleep affects students
viii Encouraging good sleep habits

Example:

Section G — *ii*

15 Section A
16 Section B

17	Section C	
18	Section D	
19	Section E	
20	Section F	

Questions 21–23
Complete the sentences below using **NO MORE THAN TWO WORDS** from Reading Passage 2 for each answer.

Write your answers in boxes 21–23.

21 When school schedules were first created, few studies had focused on pupils' …

22 During adolescence, people's sleep requirements generally increase by …

23 In a UK study, changing the school schedule led to fewer students missing school due to…

Questions 24–27
Choose the correct letter, A, B, C or D.

Write the correct letter **A–D** in answer boxes 24–27.

24 The writer expresses doubt that

    A school schedules were originally the same as they are today.

    B educational experts understand the issues involved in creating academic calendars.

    C educational issues determined how authorities originally planned the school day.

    D the school day is long enough for teenage students.

IELTS Academic Reading

25 What happens to people's natural sleep patterns during adolescence?

   A   People feel tired no matter how much sleep they get.
   B   Physical changes make people more tired during the day.
   C   People feel sleepy for shorter amounts of time.
   D   There is a delay in the time that people start to feel sleepy.

26 The writer says that parents should

   A   limit teenagers' use of electronic devices at night.
   B   give teenagers the freedom to decide their own bedtimes.
   C   encourage teenagers to go to bed earlier.
   D   set good examples by improving their own sleep routines.

27 Which statement best describes the writer's attitude towards starting the school day later?

   A   More research needs to be done to discover whether it has any drawbacks.
   B   It is worth doing despite the practical challenges it presents.
   C   The social impacts will be greater than the health benefits.
   D   It will have little impact on teenagers' academic performance.

READING PASSAGE 3

You should spend about 20 minutes on Questions 28–40, which are based on Reading Passage 3 below.

Spotlight on … Psychology

Personal insights

If you're interested in human behaviour, then a degree in psychology may be the course for you. This fascinating subject explores how mental processes work, and the various factors influencing how people act, think or feel. Psychology students gain a deep understanding of people's emotional needs, which is vital for establishing and maintaining positive relationships. At the same time, understanding how the human mind works can help people to make sense of their own emotional needs. There's no doubt that psychology is an excellent choice if your main priority is personal development.

Building your future

Of course, given the substantial financial commitment, most students choose their degree course based on factors that extend beyond opportunities for personal growth. For a degree to be an excellent investment in your future, it must equip you with transferable skills. Psychology is one of the most popular subjects to study at university precisely because it provides students with an impressive range of skills which can be used in a range of professional contexts.

Unsurprisingly, psychology graduates can communicate effectively in a range of situations, and this ability is highly desirable to employers. Psychology degrees also train participants to analyse statistical information effectively and apply critical reasoning when evaluating written information. Of course, many degrees can enhance students' analytical skills, but, due to the nature of the subject, psychology students are more likely to conduct their own research. Consequently, psychology graduates have excellent project-management skills, along with practical experience of using research tools and evaluating different types of evidence.

In short, psychology degrees equip students with numerous skills that serve them well beyond graduation.

Flexibility and range

There's no doubt that psychology is a degree subject which is extremely broad in scope. No two psychology courses are identical because of all the different modules that programmes offer. For instance, you may explore different areas including sports psychology, educational psychology, experimental psychology and many more. What adds to the flexibility of a psychology degree is that it complements a number of other subjects. Many students combine psychology with a related subject such as criminology or sociology. These combinations work well because they enable students to look at issues from different perspectives. Alternatively, many students choose to study foreign languages alongside psychology, as this can boost their career options even further.

Choosing the right course

With so many options available, your choice of course may depend on your career goals. If you have clear aspirations to work in clinical practice, then look for programmes that offer you the chance to work toward professional accreditation. These courses provide content that meets the requirements set out by professional bodies, which can help you to gain professional qualifications. Otherwise, it's worth considering a general psychology programme that offers students a variety of study options.

Careers in psychology

A degree in psychology can open up an astonishing variety of professional opportunities. Here are just a few of the exciting careers that you could pursue with a psychology degree:

- **Human Resources (HR)**
  HR managers play a vital role in every company and organisation, as they are responsible for the wellbeing of employees. They use their knowledge of motivation and conflict resolution to ensure that the workplace is healthy and productive for everyone.

- **Marketing and communications**
  Psychology graduates can build stimulating careers in marketing since they have the skills required to identify consumers' needs and feelings, and can use this to develop the most appropriate ways to develop a cohesive brand message.

- **Clinical research**
  The analytical skills that are a key feature of psychology degrees are vital in clinical research. Clinical researchers design and conduct clinical studies. These studies are used to develop treatments to help people with a wide range of disorders or problems.

- **Performance coaching**
  In both business and sporting contexts, performance coaching is all about identifying obstacles that are preventing an individual from unlocking their full potential. There are many opportunities in this emerging field, especially for graduates with knowledge of sports psychology.

- **Criminal profiling**
  Criminal profilers work in law enforcement. They analyse criminal cases and crime scenes to identify specific behavioural clues. Using this information, they create a psychological profile to assist police investigators. One of the most common routes into this career is by studying a joint degree in psychology and criminology.

Admission requirements

Since the subject is so popular, there is usually fierce competition for psychology places. As a result, most universities expect applicants to have achieved good school grades, or, alternatively, to be able to demonstrate strong academic potential. Many universities prefer applicants with biology or mathematics qualifications, but, again, this isn't compulsory. As psychology degrees begin with compulsory introductory modules, applicants are not expected to have studied the subject before. In fact, psychology attracts a wide range of applicants of all ages and educational backgrounds. If you're motivated and determined, you'll find your ideal psychology programme!

Questions 28–34

Do the following statements agree with the information in Reading Passage 3?

In boxes 28–34, write:

TRUE   If the statement agrees with the information in the passage
FALSE   If the statement contradicts the information in the passage
NOT GIVEN   If there is no information on this in the passage

28 The main reason why people choose psychology degrees is for personal growth.

29 Psychology degrees can be more expensive than other degrees.

30 Research is a common feature of psychology degrees.

31 Most psychology degrees include similar modules.

32 General psychology courses are less challenging than professional accreditation courses.

33 Performance coaching is growing in popularity.

34 Prior subject knowledge is generally required before students can enter psychology degree programmes.

Questions 35–39

Answer the questions below using **NO MORE THAN THREE WORDS** from the passage for each answer.

Write your answers in boxes 35–39.

35 What term in the text refers to abilities used in many professional roles?

36 Which additional subject is commonly chosen by students who wish to improve their job prospects?

37 What professional field do accreditation courses prepare students for?

38 Which career is concerned with the welfare of people within workplaces?

39 Which combination of subjects is popular with people who become profilers?

Question 40
What is the writer's purpose in Reading Passage 3?
Choose the correct letter, A, B, C or D.

*Write the correct letter **A–D** in the answer box below.*

A To argue for universities to widen the focus of their psychology programmes

B To describe the university admissions process for psychology applicants

C To highlight the benefits that can be gained from studying psychology

D To compare the pros and cons of different types of psychology course

Answer key

IELTS Academic Reading

Test 1

Reading Passage 1, Questions 1–14

1. iii
2. viii
3. v
4. vi
5. iv
6. FALSE
7. TRUE
8. NOT GIVEN
9. TRUE
10. FALSE
11. NOT GIVEN
12. smell a rat
13. a trillion / one trillion
14. hippocampus / the hippocampus

Reading Passage 2, Questions 15–27

15. F
16. C
17. E
18. B
19. G
20. C
21. A
22. D
23. soil / any soil
24. tank / water tank
25. nutrients / essential nutrients
26. excess water
27. B

Reading Passage 3, Questions 28–40

28. C
29. A
30. B
31. B
32. D
33. A
34. D
35. sky / night sky
36. Jewish cartographers
37. Mercator projection
38. cartographic propaganda
39. art
40. programming languages

Answers

Test 2

Reading Passage 1, Questions 1–13

1. NOT GIVEN
2. YES
3. NO
4. YES
5. NO
6. NO
7. NOT GIVEN
8. YES
9. B
10. F
11. E
12. A
13. B

Reading Passage 2, Questions 14–27

14 & 15   (in either order) B / D
16–18   (in any order) A / D / F
19. economy improves
20. American households
21. remain constant
22. peak car
23. distance travelled
24. TRUE
25. NOT GIVEN
26. FALSE
27. TRUE

Reading Passage 3, Questions 28–40

28. D
29. J
30. A
31. F
32. H
33. C
34. the Italian Renaissance / Italian Renaissance
35. lighting
36. walkways
37. promenade
38. C
39. F
40. A

IELTS Academic Reading

Test 3

Reading Passage 1, Questions 1–14

1. NO
2. NOT GIVEN
3. YES
4. NO
5. NOT GIVEN
6. YES
7. YES
8. NOT GIVEN
9. B
10. C
11. A
12. D
13. cash
14. (fundraising / charity) events

Reading Passage 2, Questions 15–27

15. v
16. vii
17. i
18. iii
19. iv
20. C
21. A
22. B
23. D
24. B
25. G
26. D
27. I

Reading Passage 3, Questions 28–40

28–31. (in any order) B / D / E / G
32. American university
33. online learning
34. literature
35. distracted
36. unfamiliar
37. FALSE
38. NOT GIVEN
39. TRUE
40. A

Answers

Test 4

Reading Passage 1, Questions 1–14

1. (as) vibrating air
2. single board computer
3. amplification
4. (the) coil
5. YES
6. NOT GIVEN
7. YES
8. NO
9–11. (in any order) A / D / E
12. data tags
13. hi fi
14. mechanical motion

Reading Passage 2, Questions 15–27

15. iv
16. viii
17. ii
18. v
19. vi
20. i
21. D
22. B
23. A
24. limited
25. conservation triage
26. keystone
27. giant panda / panda

Reading Passage 3, Questions 28–40

28. C
29. G
30. J
31. B
32. E
33. D
34. B
35. thirty / 30
36. work placement / a work placement
37. Translation
38. the Academic Office / Academic Office
39. outstanding academic credentials
40. A

IELTS Academic Reading

Test 5

Reading Passage 1, Questions 1–14

1. iii
2. vii
3. viii
4. v
5. ii
6. iv
7. YES
8. NO
9. NOT GIVEN
10. NO
11. H
12. A
13. C
14. G

Reading Passage 2, Questions 15–27

15. resource management
16. raw materials
17. once
18. recycled
19. waste
20. D
21. B
22. A
23. A
24. 130 / approximately 130
25. environmental programmes
26. compensatory behaviour
27. D

Reading Passage 3, Questions 28–40

28. D
29. A
30. C
31. F
32. E
33. B
34. F
35. public policy
36. shrimp / shrimps
37. omega-3 fatty acids
38. a week / one week
39. to be regulated / regulated
40. C

Answers

Test 6

Reading Passage 1, Questions 1–14

1. positively
2. rejection
3. adjustment
4. cultural differences
5. comfortable
6. linear
7. D
8. B
9. A
10. opportunities
11. the 1950s
12. unrealistic expectations
13. normal
14. C

Reading Passage 2, Questions 15–27

15. F
16. D
17. B
18. C
19. G
20. TRUE
21. FALSE
22. NOT GIVEN
23. TRUE
24. living in London / in London
25. preserve nature
26. improve air quality
27. level of pain / pain

Reading Passage 3, Questions 28–40

28. vi
29. i
30. iii
31. viii
32. vii
33. iv
34. ceramics / pottery
35. (a) colleague
36. gold
37. crack / (the) crack style
38. B
39. C
40. A

IELTS Academic Reading

Test 7

Reading Passage 1, Questions 1–14

1	saturated
2	land
3	cooking
4	120
5	almond
6	bee
7	TRUE
8	NOT GIVEN
9	TRUE
10	FALSE
11	FALSE
12	20% / 20 per cent
13	heating and lighting
14	B

Reading Passage 2, Questions 15–27

15	ii
16	ix
17	vi
18	iii
19	vii
20	i
21	iv
22–24	(in any order) A/C/E
25	market research
26	large sums
27	business degrees

Reading Passage 3, Questions 28–40

28	E
29	F
30	H
31	D
32	C
33	C
34	D
35	B
36	A
37	nuisance
38	integrating
39	weather
40	are consulted

Answers

Test 8

Reading Passage 1, Questions 1–14

1. D
2. A
3. B
4. C
5. B
6. NOT GIVEN
7. NO
8. NOT GIVEN
9. YES
10. YES
11. F
12. B
13. C
14. I

Reading Passage 2, Questions 15–27

15. v
16. i
17. vii
18. vi
19. iii
20. viii
21. learning needs
22. one hour
23. illness
24. C
25. D
26. A
27. B

Reading Passage 3, Questions 28–40

28. FALSE
29. NOT GIVEN
30. TRUE
31. FALSE
32. NOT GIVEN
33. TRUE
34. FALSE
35. transferable skills
36. languages / foreign languages
37. clinical practice
38. Human resources / HR
39. psychology and criminology / criminology and psychology
40. C

IELTS Reading Practice: Academic Student Book

Each of the 14 units introduces a different reading task that you may encounter during the IELTS Academic Reading test:

1. Matching headings
2. True / False / | Yes / No / Not Given
3. Matching information
4. Summary completion
5. Sentence completion
6. Multiple choice
7. Matching features
8. Choosing a title
9. Categorisation/classification
10. Matching sentence endings
11. Table completion
12. Flowchart completion
13. Diagram completion
14. Short answer questions

Each unit contains three two-page sections:

1. Think and prepare starts with some questions to get you thinking about the unit topic, and introduces some challenging words and phrases that will appear in the practice activities that follow.

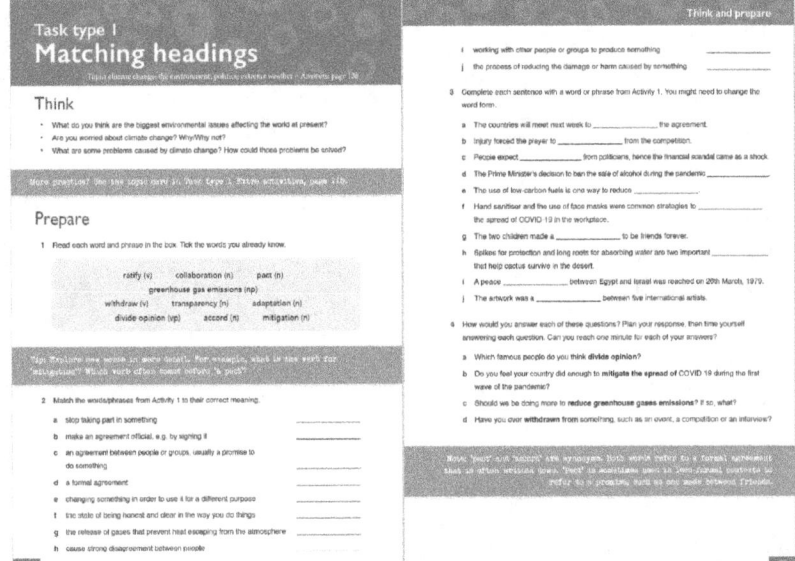

2. Practise introduces a new reading task for you to practise the task type using a text that is shorter than what will feature in the exam. It starts with some strategies and tips for how to approach each task, for you to try these strategies out during the activities then reflect on what went well, what you learned and what you will need to do to improve.

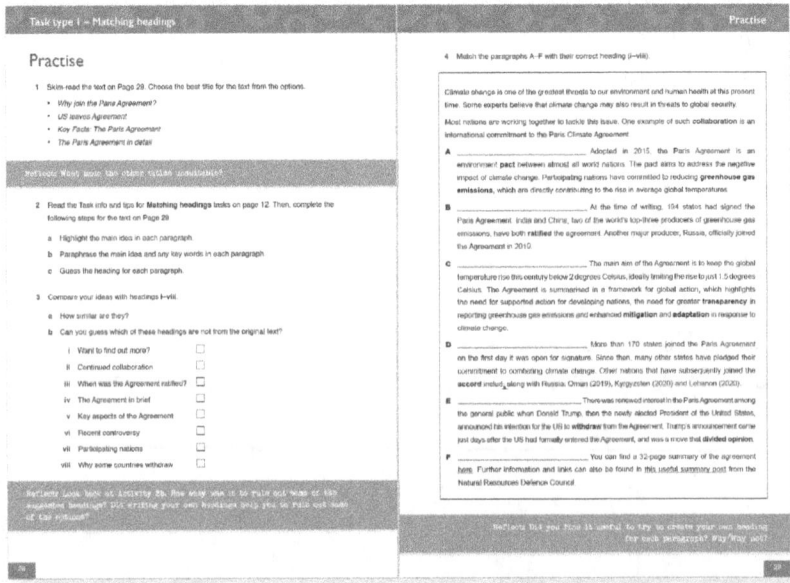

3. Put it to the test includes a text that is designed to replicate an IELTS Reading test task. There is no support here – it's just you, the text and the questions!

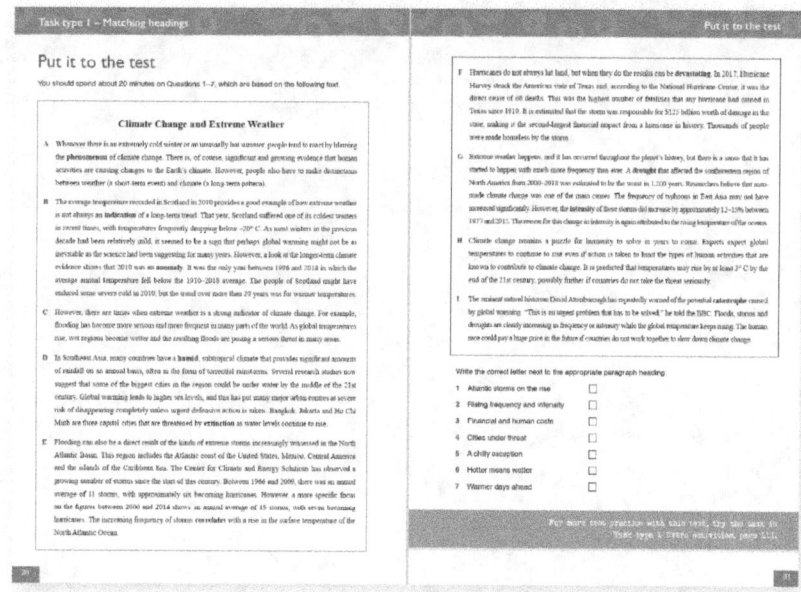

Appendices:

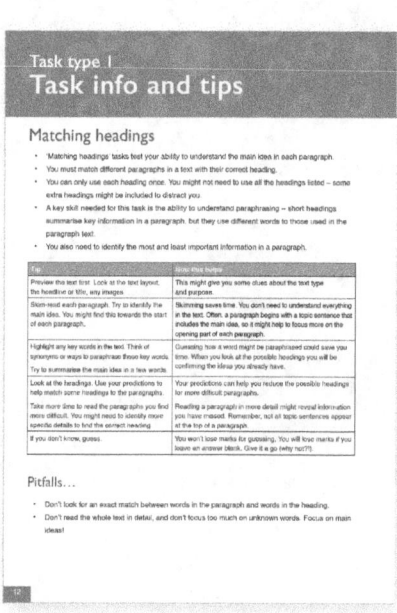

Task info and tips:
Definitions of each task type, and tips on how to approach the task.

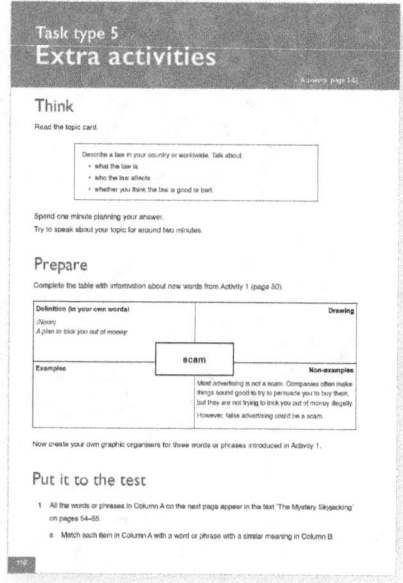

Extra activities:
Further practice in applying different task types to the units' texts.

Answers:
Comprehensive answers and guidance for each activity.

Glossary and Index:
Definitions of all high-level vocabulary used.